EXPLOITS

THE CHRONICLES OF LUCIFER JONES

Volume I—1922-1926: Adventures

Volume II—1926-1931: Exploits

Volume III—1931-1934: Encounters

Volume IV—1934-1938: Hazards
(*published by Subterranean Press*)

Volume V—1938-1942: Voyages
(*forthcoming from Subterranean Press*)

THE CHRONICLES OF LUCIFER JONES

VOLUME II 1926-1931

EXPLOITS

MIKE RESNICK

an imprint of

MANOR

Rockville, Maryland

ISBN: 978-1-61242-035-6

www.PhoenixPick.com

**Great Science Fiction & Fantasy
Free Ebook Every Month**

**Visit the Author's Website
http://MikeResnick.com**

Published by Phoenix Pick
an imprint of Arc Manor
P. O. Box 10339
Rockville, MD 20849-0339
www.ArcManor.com

To Carol, as always,

And to my father, William Resnick, who initiated
a chain of events half a century ago that
culminated in the publication of this book.

♈

CONTENTS

CAST OF CHARACTERS   9

1. THE MASTER DETECTIVE   11

2. THE SIN CITY DERBY   26

3. THE INSIDIOUS ORIENTAL DENTIST   43

4. THE GREAT WALL   57

5. THE ABOMINABLE SNOWMAN   71

6. THE LAND OF ETERNAL YOUTH   82

7. SECRET SEX   94

8. THE FLAME OF BHARATPUR   108

9. THE SCORPION LADY   122

10. THE OTHER MASTER DETECTIVE   136

CAST OF CHARACTERS

Inspector Willie Wong, who has run out of names for his sons, and possesses a platitude for every occasion.

General Chang, a warlord's warlord.

Doctor Aristotle Ho, the Insidious Oriental Dentist, who plans to take over the world or lower south Brooklyn, whichever comes first.

Rupert Cornwall, a scoundrel with a passion for rubies, wealthy women, and duplicity.

Harvey Edwards, former halfback, now the fastest rickshaw puller in Macau.

Mr. Mako, diminutive Japanese detective who specializes in judo, disguise, archaeology and jealousy.

Cuddles, an authentic Chinese dragon.

The Scorpion Lady, a beautiful but deadly smuggler with a truly outstanding pair of lungs.

Sir Mortimer Edgerton-Smythe, who will stop at nothing to bring Doctor Aristotle Ho to justice.

Sam Hightower, a semi-abominable Snowman who is hiding out from the mob in the mountains of Tibet.

Capturing Clyde Calhoun, world-famous hunter who brings 'em back alive. Not intact, but alive.

Lisara, a 111-year-old virgin who has taken up the High Priestess trade.

Akbar, a learning-disabled elephant.

Lady Edith Quilton, the richest widow lady in Rajasthan Province.

And our narrator, *The Right Reverend Honorable Doctor Lucifer Jones*, a handsome, noble and resourceful Christian gentleman who has certain unresolved disagreements with eight separate Asian governments over the finer points of the law.

1. THE MASTER DETECTIVE

They say that there are a lot of differences between Hong Kong and some of the African cities I had recently left behind. Different people, different cultures, different buildings, even different food.

Of course, there are a lot of similarities, too. Same lack of consideration for those who are bold enough to tinker with the laws of statistical probability. Same steel bars in the local jail. Same concrete walls and floors. Same uncomfortable cots. Same awful food.

Truth to tell, I'd had a lot more time to consider the similarities than the differences. I'd gotten right off the boat from Portuguese East Africa, checked into the Luk Kwok Hotel (which thoughtfully rented its rooms by the hour, the night, or the week), spent the next hour in a local restaurant trying to down a bowl of soup with a pair of chopsticks, and then, realizing that my funds needed replenishing, I got involved in a friendly little game of chance involving two cubes of ivory with spots painted on them. It was when a third cube slipped out of my sleeve that I was invited to inspect the premises of the local jail.

That had been five days ago, and I had spent the intervening time alternately trying not to mind the smell of dead fish, which is what all of Hong Kong smelled like back in 1926, and gaining some comfort by reading my well-worn copy of the Good Book, which I ain't never without.

The girl that brought my grub to me was a charming little thing named Mei Sung. She was right impressed to be serving a man of the cloth, which I was back in those days, and I converted the bejabbers out of her three or four times a day, which made my incarceration in durance vile a mite easier to take.

As time crawled by I got to know my fellow inmates. There was a Turkish dentist who had gassed a British officer to death in what he assured me was an accident and would certainly have been construed as such by the courts if he hadn't appropriated the officer's wallet and wristwatch before reporting the poor fellow's untimely demise. There was a young Brazilian student who sweated up a storm and kept screaming things about anarchy and tyrants and such and keeping everyone awake. There were two Chinamen dressed all in black, who kept glaring at me every time I finished converting Mei Sung. There was a Frenchman who kept saying he was glad he had killed the chef, and that anyone who ruined *sole almondine* that badly deserved to die.

And there was me, the Right Reverend Honorable Doctor Lucifer Jones, out of Moline, Illinois by way of the Dark Continent, where I'd done my best to illuminate the dark, dreary lives of the godless black heathen despite certain minor disagreements with the constabularies of fourteen countries which culminated in my being asked to establish the Tabernacle of Saint Luke on some other land mass. But I already wrote that story, and I ain't going to go into it again, since anyone who's read it knows that I'm a righteous and God-fearing man who was just misunderstood.

On the fifth day of the thirty that I was to serve, they gave me a roommate, a well-dressed Australian with expensive-looking rings on all his fingers. His name was Rupert Cornwall, and he explained that he had come to Hong Kong because Australia was a pretty empty country and he liked crowds.

"And what do you do for a living, Brother Rupert?" I asked him, by way of being polite.

"I'm an entrepreneur," he said. "I put opportunists together with opportunities, and take a little percentage for my trouble."

"I didn't know being an entrepreneur was a criminal offense in Hong Kong," I said.

"I was arrested by mistake," he answered.

"You, too?"

"Absolutely," he said. "I expect to be out of here within the hour. And what about yourself? You look like a man of God with that turned-around collar of yours."

"You hit the nail right on the head, Brother Rupert. That's what I am: a man of God, here to bring comfort and spiritual uplifting to the heathen."

"What religion do you belong to?" he asked.

"One me and the Lord worked out betwixt ourselves one Sunday afternoon back in Illinois," I said. "Hell, the way I see it, as long as we're upright and holy and got a poorbox, what's the difference?"

He broke out into a great big smile. "I *like* you, Dr. Jones," he said. "Where's your church located?"

"Well, I ain't quite got around to building my tabernacle yet, Brother Rupert...but I'm taking donations for it, if the spirit's come upon you and you're so inclined."

"I don't have any money with me," he answered. "But look me up after we're both out of here, and I might have some work for you."

"Work wasn't exactly what I had in mind," I said distastefully.

"When you hear what I have to offer, you might change your mind," he said.

"Yeah?"

He nodded. "I could use a man of the cloth in my operation. I think we could enter into a mutually profitable relationship."

"You don't say?" I replied. "Well, I suppose I could always take a brief fling at the entrepreneur business before I erect my tabernacle, God being the patient and understanding soul that He is."

He reached into his vest pocket and handed me his card. "That's my business address. Remember to call on me."

Well, I could tell we were hitting it off right fine, and I was going to ask him more about our pending partnership, but just then a guard came by and unlocked the door.

"They made your bail again, Rupert," he said in a bored voice.

"Was there every any doubt?" asked Rupert smugly.

"You get arrested by mistake a lot?" I asked as he was leaving.

"Almost daily," he said. "Personally, I think they're just jealous of my success."

Then he was gone, and I was left with my thoughts until Mei Sung came by for another conversion, which left me so exhausted that I thought I might grab a quick forty winks. I had snored my way through about twenty of 'em when the door opened again, and the guard gestured me to follow him.

"Did somebody make my bail, too?" I asked, thinking of Rupert Cornwall. He just chuckled and kept leading me down one corridor after another until we finally came to a little cubbyhole, which was filled with a desk, two chairs, and a pudgy Chinaman with a natty little mustache and goatee. He was dressed in a white linen suit, and hadn't bothered to take his Panama hat off even though we were inside.

"Sit, please," he said, smiling at me.

I sat myself down in the empty chair while he nodded at the guard, who left the room.

"You are Mr. Jones?" said the Chinaman.

"Doctor Lucifer Jones at your service," I said.

"That what we must talk about," he said in pigeon English.

"About whether I'm Lucifer Jones?" I asked, puzzled.

"About whether you are at my service," he said. "Because if not, then you go back to cell for twenty-five more days."

"Are you the guy who made my bail?" I asked.

"No one make your bail," he said. "Please sit back and relax, Doctor Jones. I am Inspector Willie Wong of Hong Kong Police Force. Perhaps you have heard of me?"

"Can't say that I have, Brother Wong," I answered. He looked right disappointed at that. "Why are you wasting your time with me, anyway?" I continued. "You ought to be trying to find the ungodly sinner that stuck that extra die up my sleeve."

"That no concern of mine," he said, holding up a hand. "But am prepared to make deal, Dr. Jones. You help me, I help you."

"Yeah?"

He nodded. "Man in your cell named Rupert Cornwall."

"What about him?"

"Rupert Cornwall biggest gangster in Hong Kong."

"Then why did you let him go?"

"Beauty is in eye of beholder," said Wong.

"I beg your pardon?"

"Old Chinese proverb. Perhaps it not translate very well." He paused. "Let Rupert Cornwall go for lack of evidence."

"What has all this got to do with me?" I asked.

"Patience, Doctor Jones," said Wong. "Penny saved is penny earned."

"Another proverb?"

He nodded. "Very wise of you to notice. You are man we need."

"Need for what, Brother Wong?" I asked.

"Need go-between. Rupert Cornwall trust you. You will meet with him, learn about operation, report back to me. Then, when time is right, we strike."

"How long you figure this'll take?"

He shrugged. "Maybe week, maybe month, who know? Too many chefs spoil the soup."

"I don't know, Brother Wong," I said. "After all, I only got twenty-five days left to serve."

He broke out into a great big grin. "You not acquainted with Chinese calendar, I take it?"

"How long is twenty-five days on a Chinese calendar?" I asked.

He shrugged again. "Maybe week, maybe month, who know?" He looked across the desk at me. "We have deal?"

I sighed. "We have a deal."

"Good. Knew I could count on man of cloth."

"How do I report to you?" I asked.

"He know what I look like, so you will report to me through sons."

"I don't know how to break this unhappy tiding to you, Brother Wong," I said, "but I ain't got no sons."

"I have twenty-eight," he replied distastefully. "All currently unemployed and available to work for honorable father."

"Twenty-eight?" I repeated. "I don't envy your missus none."

"Have seventeen missuses," he answered. "Fifteen currently suing for back alimony. That's why move here from Honolulu."

"My heart bleeds for you, Brother Wong," I said with as much sincerity as I could muster on the spur of the moment.

"Whenever I become depressed over situation, I just remember old Chinese proverb: Watched pot never boil." He got to his feet and walked around the desk to stand in front of me. "I think for this case we use Number Nine and Number Twenty-Six sons."

"What are their names?"

"Just told you: Nine and Twenty-Six. Ran out of names after Number Five son was born."

"What do you call your daughters—A through Z?"

Wong threw back his head and laughed. "You fine fellow, Doctor Jones. Wonderful sense of humor. Sincerely hope Rupert Cornwall not cut your tongue out before case is over."

"Uh…let's just pause a second for serious reflection, Brother Wong," I said. "Old Rupert wouldn't really cut my tongue out, would he?"

"No, not really," said Wong.

"That's better."

"Would have one of his hired killers do it for him."

"You know," I said, "upon further consideration, I think the Lord would want me to serve out my full sentence. After all, I was caught fair and square, and somehow this seems unfair to the just and honorable man who sentenced me."

"Whatever you say, Doctor Jones," said Wong. He went back around the desk, opened the drawer, and pulled out a sheet of paper that was subdivided into hundreds of little squares. "This help you pass the time."

"What is it?" I asked.

He smiled. "Calendar of Chinese week." He tossed me a pencil. "You can mark off each day with this. Will bring new one when you run out of lead."

Which is how I became an operative in the employ of the Hong Kong Police.

You'd think that the biggest gangster in Hong Kong would operate out of one of them beautiful old palaces that overlook the ocean, or failing that he'd set up headquarters in a penthouse suite in some luxury hotel. So you can imagine my surprise when I wandered down a couple of back alleyways and found Rupert Cornwall's place of business to be a rundown little storefront right between a fish peddler and a shirtmaker.

The whole area smelled of incense and dead fish, and there were lots of tall men dressed in black and wearing lean and hungry looks, but I just ignored 'em all like the God-fearing Christian gentleman that I am and walked up to Cornwall's door and pounded on it a couple of times. A muscular guy, who looked like a cross between an Olympic weightlifter and a small mountain, let me in and ushered me through a maze of unopened cardboard boxes to a back room, where Rupert Cornwall sat in an easy chair, smoking a Havana cigar and going through the Hong Kong version of the *Daily Racing Form*.

"Doctor Jones!" he said. "My dear fellow, I hadn't expected to see you again for almost a month!" He paused and looked around. "We just moved in here a few days ago. I used to operate out of one of the hotels, but my overhead was killing me."

"Yeah, I know how expensive them luxury suites can be," I agreed.

"Luxury suites nothing," he corrected me. "It was making bail two and three times a day. Ah, well, you're here, and that's all that matters." Suddenly his eyes narrowed. "Just how, exactly, did you get here so soon?"

"I'm a fast walker, Brother Rupert," I answered.

"I thought you were incarcerated for 30 days."

I shrugged. "Time flies when you're having fun. I guess I'd been there longer than I thought."

"Yes, I saw little Mei Sung," he said with a grin. "Well, are you prepared to discuss the details of our first business venture?"

"That's what I'm here for, Brother Rupert," I said.

"Fine," he said. "I want you to know up front that I am an honest businessman who would never dream of harming another soul, Dr. Jones."

"I could tell that right off," I said.

"I seek no commendation for my work," he continued. "I'm in the import/export business, hardly a noteworthy or romantic occupation. I pay my bills on time, I treat my help well, I have virtually no social life, I avoid the spotlight at all costs. In point of fact, I am a *laissez-faire* capitalist of the highest order. And yet, there is a local official who has harassed me, threatened me, tried to drive me out of business, and caused me a considerable loss of revenue."

"No!" I said, shocked.

"Yes, Dr. Jones," he replied. "I have borne his enmity silently up to now, but he has become an intolerable nuisance, and it is my intention to so embarrass him that he is forced to resign from his position, if not leave Hong Kong altogether."

"What does this have to do with *me*, Brother Rupert?" I asked.

"I cannot proceed with my plan alone. For your complicity in ridding me of this vile and obdurate man, I am willing to pay you the sum of one thousand British pounds sterling. What do you say to that?"

"That's a right tidy sum," I allowed. "Just who is this here villain that we plan to put out of commission?"

"A man named Wong."

"Would that be Inspector Willie Wong of the Hong Kong Police?" I suggested.

"The very same. How is it that you come to know his name, Dr. Jones?"

"Oh, they bandy it around a lot down at the jail," I said.

"Have you any compunctions in helping me rid decent society of this man?"

"Not a one," I said. "Why, did you know that every single man he arrested swore that he was innocent? We certainly can't have a man like that riding roughshod over the people of this fair city."

He broke out into a great big smile. "I believe we understand each other perfectly, Doctor Jones. I *knew* I had selected the right man!"

"How do we plan to deal with this menace to social stability and free enterprise?" I asked.

"Willie Wong's reputation rests on the fact that he has never made a mistake, never arrested an innocent man, never let a guilty one get away," said Cornwall, puffing on his cigar. "If we can publicly embarrass and humiliate him, I believe his honor will demand that he retire from public service."

"And just how do we aim to do that?"

"I have it on good authority that the Empire Emerald, the largest gemstone in all of China, will be stolen from the Fung Ping Shan Museum tomorrow night," he said, leaning forward in his chair. "I will arrange that every clue points toward you, and knowing Wong, he will almost certainly bring you into custody within hours of the robbery. It will then be revealed that he has wrongly arrested a man of God, and that, furthermore, the emerald was stolen by one of his own sons." He leaned back with a satisfied smile. "What do you think of that?"

"I think I want five hundred pounds up front and the name of a good bondsman, just in case something goes wrong," I said.

"Certainly, my dear Doctor Jones." He pulled out a wallet thick enough to choke a small elephant and peeled off five one-hundred-pound notes, which he then handed over to me. "I distrust a man who doesn't look out for his own interest."

"Okay," I said, stuffing the money into my pocket. "What else do I have to know or do?"

"Very little," he said. "Spend an hour browsing at the museum late tomorrow afternoon, perhaps get into a slight altercation with one of the tourists so people will remember seeing you there, keep off the streets between midnight and two o'clock in the morning, and put *this* in a safe place."

With that, he handed me a small cloth bag that was closed with a drawstring.

"What's in it?" I asked.

"Take a look."

I opened it up, and found a lump of coal about the size of a golf ball.

"*That*, Doctor Jones, will prove to be the undoing of Willie Wong. Hide it well, but not so well that a thorough search cannot turn it up. While you are spending the night in jail and his men are ransacking your room, my own operatives will plant the real emerald on one of his brats."

"An emerald this big is an awful high price to pay to get rid of one bothersome policeman," I said.

"He costs me more than that every week," said Cornwall. "It will be money well spent."

"Well, considering that it ain't yours to begin with, I reckon I can see the logic in that," I agreed.

"And now, Doctor Jones, it is best that we part company. I don't want anyone to know that we've been in contact since my release from jail." He stood up and walked me to the door. "Your remaining five hundred pounds will be delivered in an envelope to your hotel the morning after your arrest, and you will be contacted later in the week concerning our next venture."

"Sounds good to me, Brother Rupert," I said, shaking his hand. "It's always nice to do business with a Christian gentleman like yourself."

"We've lots more business to do when this sordid little affair is over," he said with a twinkle in his eye.

I kind of doubted it, since he never asked me what hotel he was supposed to deliver my money to. But with five hundred pounds in my pocket and Willie Wong on my side, I decided that things were definitely looking up for the Tabernacle of Saint Luke.

I had walked maybe half a mile from Cornwall's office when I saw two young Chinamen staring at me from a street corner, so I strolled over to them.

"Nine?" I said to the bigger one.

There was no response.

"Twenty-Six?" I said.

"Make it thirty and you've got yourself a date," he said with a giggle.

"Doctor Jones!" yelled a young man from across the street. "We're over here!"

I turned and saw two more Chinamen and made a beeline toward them.

"Are you Willie Wong's kids?" I asked.

The older one nodded. "We've got orders to take you to Dad."

"Lead the way," I said.

I followed them a couple of blocks to a dimly-lit restaurant. They left me at the door, and as I entered it I saw Wong nod to me from a table in the back.

"You visit with Mr. Rupert Cornwall, yes?" he said, gesturing me to sit down.

"Yeah. He doesn't like you much."

"Stitch in time save nine."

"You ever consider writing a Chinese proverb book?" I asked him.

"Please continue," he said, slurping his soup.

"Near as I can make out, he plans to steal the Empire Emerald around midnight tomorrow."

"Ah, so."

"Not only that," I added. "But he plans to make it look like *I* stole it, and while you're busy arresting me he's going to plant it on one of your sons."

"Very interesting," he said with no show of interest whatsoever.

"Well, that's it. I'm done now, right?" I said. "I mean, you'll be waiting for him at the museum, and I can go off converting all you godless yellow heathen—no offense intended—and maybe build my tabernacle."

"Not that easy," said Wong.

"Why not?" I demanded.

"Cannot make omelet without breaking eggs."

"What the hell is that supposed to mean?"

"So sorry," he said. "Wrong proverb." He paused and tried again. "Beauty only skin deep."

"Well, that explains everything," I said.

"Cannot capture Mr. Rupert Cornwall at museum where emerald reside," continued Wong as he finished his soup.

"I already told you what time he's going to show up."

"*He* will not steal emerald. He will have underling do so. I do not want little fish while big fish lead horse to water but cannot make him drink."

"So what *do* you plan to do?"

"Mr. Rupert Cornwall expect me to arrest you. I will not disappoint him."

"That may not disappoint *him*," I said, "but it'll disappoint the hell out of *me*."

He shook his head. "Just go through motions. Then catch him when he try to plant emerald on honorable son."

"What if he has a henchman do *that*, too?" I asked.

"Almost certainly will. After all, home is where heart is."

"I don't think you understand me, Brother Wong," I said. "What's the difference if you catch a henchman stealing the emerald or you catch one planting it on your kid?"

"Much easier to trace emerald back to Mr. Rupert Cornwall *after* he has stolen it than before," explained Wong.

"And what happens to me?" I asked.

"We arrest you with much fanfare in afternoon, release you when we apprehend henchman that night."

Then a particularly bothersome thought occurred to me. "What if he changes his mind and decides to keep the emerald?"

"Then you have lied to me, I take full credit for capturing you, city give another medal to humble detective, and I apprehend Mr. Rupert Cornwall some other day." He smiled. "You see, either way it all work out."

Well, I could see it all working out for Willie Wong and Rupert Cornwall a lot easier than it all working out for me, so me and the Lord decided that it was time to take matters into our own hands, and what we did was this: I went out shopping at a bunch of costume jewelry stores, and when I finally came to a fake emerald about the size of the lump of coal I was toting around in the little cloth bag, I bought it for twenty pounds and tucked it away in my pocket.

Then I went over to Bonham Road and visited the Fung Ping Shan Museum a day early, found the Empire Emerald, and tried to figure out how to substitute my stone for the real one, but since I'm a God-fearing Christian missionary who ain't never had an illegal impulse in my life, I finally had to admit that while the trip wires and the lock on the front door wouldn't give me no problems, the alarm built into the case was a type I hadn't seen before and there was just no way I was going to be able to switch the emeralds without setting it off and waking up such dead as weren't otherwise occupied at the time.

One thing I did notice, though, was that the guards were Brits and not Chinamen, so I waited until they locked up the museum and followed one of them home. I got his name off the mailbox, and early the next morning, right after he'd left for work, I called his wife and told her that my laundry shop had inadvertently ruined her husband's tuxedo, but that we would be happy to make amends. She explained that he didn't *have* a tuxedo, and I told her I was sure it was his but just to make doubly certain I needed to know the name of the establishment she did her business with, and as soon as she told me I popped over there and informed them I was a visiting relative who had been sent by to pick up any uniforms he might have left there. Sure enough, they had one, all bright and green and neatly pressed, with shining brass buttons. I tipped them a couple of pounds, took it to the men's room in the back of a nearby tavern, and slipped it on—and an hour later I was patrolling the corridors of the museum, nodding pleasantly to passersby and keeping a watchful eye on the emerald.

Then, when the museum hit a slow period and the room containing the Empire Emerald had emptied out, I walked into it with a beer in my hand, set it down atop the glass case that covered the gemstone, and tipped the bottle over. I pulled the phony emerald out of my pocket, lifted up the glass cover, and as the alarm went off I quickly exchanged it for the real emerald, got down on my knees, pulled out a handkerchief, and set about trying to clean the beer off the glass.

The room filled up to overflowing with guards about ten seconds later. A couple of them even covered me with their pistols until they saw the emerald where it ought to be, and then they helped me put the glass cover back on. I explained that I was new on the job, and that I was just trying to clean up after myself because I had spilled some beer, and after telling me what a clumsy fool I was, they told me to pack up my gear and go home, that my services were no longer needed. They managed to get the alarm turned off just about the time I was climbing down the museum steps to the sidewalk in front of the building.

I went back to my room at the Luk Kwok Hotel, where I had a little chat with my Silent Partner, explaining to Him that while what I did may have seemed a criminal act on the surface of it, if He would examine the consequences carefully He would have to agree that it was for the best all the way around. Willie Wong was still going to capture Rupert Cornwall, so *he* would be happy; the museum would never know they weren't displaying the real Empire Emerald, so *they* would be happy; Cornwall was going to go to jail anyway, so at least he wouldn't be any *less* happy for not having the emerald in his possession for a couple of minutes. And me, I finally had sufficient capital to build the Tabernacle of Saint Luke, which I promised the Lord I would do just as soon as I spent a few years scouting out the territory for the very best location.

Everything went pretty smoothly the next day. First thing I did was stop by the laundry and drop off the uniform, so no one would notice it was missing and maybe start thinking about *why* it was missing. Then I scouted up some lunch that didn't smell of fish, and wandered the streets a bit, and at about two in the afternoon I walked over to the museum, lingered there for an hour or two, had a very public misunderstanding with a blonde Frenchwoman, and then headed back toward the Luk Kwok.

Along the way, I picked up some chewing gum and stuck a wad of it into my mouth. Then I stopped by a little gift shop, and while the proprietor was speaking to another customer, I stuck the Empire Emerald on the back of his radiator with the chewing gum. Since it was mid-summer, I knew he wasn't going to fiddle with the radiator for another few months, and I figured to be back for it within just a day or two. The very last thing I did was hide the cloth bag with the lump of coal inside the water tank behind the toilet once I returned to room in the Luk Kwok. Then I lay back on my bed, pulled out the Good Book, and whiled the night away reading about Solomon's more exotic dalliances.

The police showed up right on schedule, at a quarter after two in the morning, and hustled me off to jail. I kept protesting my innocence, the way I figured both Willie Wong and Rupert Cornwall would expect of me, and then, just after daybreak, a guard came and unlocked my cell. As far as I was concerned he could have waited another couple of hours, since I hadn't yet got around to converting Mei Sung again, but given the circumstances I didn't think it proper to protest, so I let him escort me to freedom, which turned out to be Wong's little cubbyhole.

"Good morning, Doctor Jones," he said without getting up from his chair.

"Good morning, Brother Wong," I said. "How'd it go last night?"

"Apprehend whole gang," he said happily. "Rupert Cornwall in cell one flight up from yours."

"That's great news, Brother Wong," I said. "And did you get the emerald back?"

"Empire Emerald once again on display in Fung Ping Shan Museum."

"I guess that closes the case."

He nodded. "Cannot teach old dog new tricks."

"Well, I'll sure remember that the next time I run into an old dog, Brother Wong," I said. "I assume I'm free to go."

"Farther you go, the better."

"I beg your pardon?"

"It best you leave Hong Kong," said Wong. "Many friends and clients of Rupert Cornwall not very pleased with you."

"A telling point," I agreed. "Gimme just a couple of hours to get my gear together and I'll be off."

"Thank you for help, Doctor Jones," said Wong. "Knew you were right man for job."

"My pleasure, Brother Wong," I said.

Then I took my leave of him, went back to the Luk Kwok, and looked around to see if there was anything I wanted to take along with me. There were some old shirts and pants and socks and such, but since I was about to pick up the Empire Emerald on my way out of town, I decided that I really owed myself a new wardrobe, so I finally left empty-handed.

I moseyed over to the area where the gift shop was, did maybe an hour of serious window-shopping up and down the street for the benefit of anyone who might have been watching me, and finally entered the little store after I was sure I wasn't being observed.

"You are Lucifer Jones, are you not?" asked the proprietor the second I closed the door behind me.

"How did you know?" I asked. "I don't recall talking to you last night."

"I was given your description by Inspector Wong," he replied. "He left a note for you."

He handed me a folded-up piece of paper, which I opened and read:

Dear Doctor Jones:

Had feeling all along you were perfect man for job. Had honorable Number Ten, Fourteen, Seventeen, and Twenty-Two sons observe you constantly since you left custody. Not only is Rupert Cornwall under arrest, but we now know weakness in museum security system, all thanks to you.

Is old Chinese custom to exchange gifts. You will know where to look for yours.

Your humble servant,

Willie Wong,
Hong Kong Police

P.S. Money is root of all evil.

I threw the paper down on the counter and raced over to the radiator. I reached behind it, found my gum and the stone, and pulled it out: it was the same lump of coal Rupert Cornwall had given me two days ago.

"Is something wrong, Mr. Jones?" asked the storekeeper.

"Nothing I shouldn't have expected from trusting someone who ain't a decent, God-fearing Christian," I said bitterly. "Give me a map, brother."

"A map?" he repeated.

"This town's seen the last of me," I said. "I'm heading to where a man of the cloth can convert souls in peace and quiet without worrying about getting flimflammed by gangsters and detectives and the like."

He pulled a map out from behind the counter. I looked at it for a minute and then, with four hundred and fifty pounds of Rupert Cornwall's money still in my pocket, I lit out across the mouth of the Pearl River for Macau, where I hoped to find a better class of sinner to listen to my preaching.

2. THE SIN CITY DERBY

Macau didn't smell a lot better than Hong Kong, and it wasn't no cleaner, but it offered more opportunities to an enterprising Christian gentleman like myself. In fact, it offered more opportunities to just about everybody, since it was where all the young Hong Kong bucks went to do their gambling and find their short-term ladyfriends.

I got off the ferry, trying to figure out what to do next, when a young blond guy pulling an empty rickshaw stopped in front of me.

"Howdy, brother," I said. "Take me to wherever it is that the white folks stay when they're in town."

"That'd be the Bela Vista Hotel," he said in perfect American. "But you can do better at the Macau Inn, over on the Travesso de Padre Narciso."

"Sounds good to me," I said, climbing into the seat. "Let 'er rip."

"I can also get you into half a dozen high-class gambling clubs," he said as he began pulling the rickshaw down the street. "And if you've got an interest in the ladies…"

"Well, mostly I'm here to raise money for my tabernacle," I said. "But I gotta admit it makes more sense to go where the money is than where it ain't. And of course, part of my calling is to show wicked, painted Jezebels the power and the glory."

He turned and grinned at me. "It sounds like you've got yourself a mighty interesting religion, Preacher," he said. "I wouldn't mind joining up myself."

"How'd a well-spoken young feller like you come to be in the rickshaw trade thousands of miles from church and home in the first place?" I asked him.

"It's a long story," he said. "But the gist of it is that I hired on to work on an archeological dig in the Gobi Desert. Our boat docked in Hong Kong on a Saturday afternoon, and a bunch of us came over to the Sin City of Macau for one last fling before going out in the wilderness."

"Makes sense," I allowed.

"They told us to be back at sun-up on Monday, which was when the truck was leaving. I guess I overslept a little."

"And they didn't wait for you?"

"I didn't get out of bed until half past Tuesday, and I figured they were all gone by then, so I looked around for some way to earn my passage back home. I thought I could be a croupier, or maybe a personal manager for some ladies of the evening, but all the good jobs were taken, and so I wound up pulling this goddamned rickshaw."

He took a hard left turn, and suddenly I could see the Macau Inn straight ahead of us.

"Here we are, Preacher," he said, sprinting the final fifty yards.

"Take it easy," I said. "We ain't in no race."

"Sorry," he said, coming to a stop in front of the hotel. "Sometimes I pretend I'm still outrunning tacklers on the football field back in high school. It helps to pass the time."

"You played football?"

"Sure did," he answered. "And being an ex-halfback gives me an edge on the competition. If we see a single customer stepping off the ferry or out of a hotel, I always get there first."

It was just about that instant that the Lord smote me right betwixt the eyes with a great big heavenly revelation.

"Are you telling me there ain't no coolie in town can match strides with you?" I said.

"Not a one," he said. "I even had a couple of Big Ten scholarship offers—until they threw me off the team for a few minor infractions, that is."

"What kind of infractions?"

"Oh…Zelda, Thelma, Patti…those kinds."

"Brother," I said. "How'd you like to get enough money for passage back to the good old U. S. of A. and have a little pocket money left over for an occasional infraction?"

"You've got a curious expression on your face, Preacher," he said. "I can't quite tell if you're joking or not."

"I never joke about money," I said. "It's against the Third and Eighth Commandments. Come on inside and let's talk a little business."

He pulled the rickshaw over to a side of the road and followed me into the Macau Inn. There was a great big fountain in the middle of the lobby, with about a dozen parrots dangling down from the ceiling in bamboo cages. There was a fat white man in a wrinkled suit and a fez talking to a couple of turbaned Indians in a corner, and an Englishman in tweeds was sitting on a leather chair, smoking a pipe and reading a copy of the *China Morning Post*. We walked past the check-in desk and turned left at the restaurant, which was just about empty, it being the middle of the afternoon.

"Have a seat," I said, escorting my rickshaw driver to a small table.

"Don't mind if I do," he replied.

"By the way, Brother, I didn't catch your name."

"Harvey," he said, reaching out and shaking my hand. "Harvey Edwards, and before we discuss any further business, you still owe me for the ride."

"How much?"

"Tell you what," he said. "Buy me a couple of beers and we'll call it square."

"I can't do that, Brother Harvey," I said, reaching into my pocket and pulling out a couple of coins. "This ought to cover what I owe you."

"You got something against beer, Preacher?" he asked.

"Not a thing," I answered. "Nothing slakes the thirst like a cold beer."

"Then what's the problem?"

"*I* ain't got no problem, Brother Harvey," I said. "But *you*—you're in training."

"For what?"

"The rickshaw races."

He frowned. "What are you talking about? There *ain't* any rickshaw races in Macau."

I grinned at him. "Yet," I said.

Suddenly his eyes lit up like little candles. "Oh?"

"Brother Harvey, I been mulling on it, and I can't see no reason why I should risk the Lord's money playing fan-tan and other games of chance with these local sharks when we can invite 'em into *our* pool."

"You know," said Harvey with a great big smile, "I can't think of any reason either."

"Good!" I said. "Then we're in business."

"Fifty-fifty," he replied.

I shook my head. "One-third for you, one-third for me, and one-third for the Lord, which is only fair, since He's putting up the money."

"He ain't doing the running, though," said Harvey adamantly.

Well, we hemmed and we hawed and we haggled, and what it finally came down to was that Harvey and I would split the first ten thousand pounds we made down the middle, and the Lord got Himself a twenty percent option on the rest, provided He produced fair weather and a fast track. That settled, we indulged in a couple of grilled Macau pigeons, and then I started asking him where we were likely to find the biggest plungers.

"No question about it," he said. "They're all at the Central Hotel."

"Never heard of it."

"You're about the first person I've run across who hasn't," said Harvey. "It's the biggest building in town, even if it *is* only nine stories tall. You can see it from just about anywhere."

"Maybe I ought to rent a room there instead of here," I suggested.

He laughed at that. "They'll be charging you rent every twenty minutes, Preacher," he said. "It ain't exactly your run-of-the-mill hotel."

Which was an understatement if ever there was one.

We waited till the sun went down and then made our way over to the Central Hotel, which despite its name wasn't a hotel at all. We walked in the main entrance, and found ourselves on the ground floor, which was crawling with coolies. There were small-stakes games of roulette and baccarat and fan-tan going on everywhere, and the girls were just about all in need of a little soap and water and a good dentist.

"These guys don't look like no high rollers to me," I said as we began walking across the room.

"They're not," replied Harvey.

"Well, then?" I asked.

"Follow me," he said, walking toward a huge, winding staircase.

The coolies were a little better-dressed on the second floor, and the girls looked a mite healthier. By the third floor, they were playing with British pounds instead of Hong Kong dollars, and we ran into a bunch of Indians on the fourth floor. When we reached the fifth floor, most of the players were Europeans and well-dressed Chinamen, and the girls were so downright beautiful that I remarked to Harvey that I couldn't wait to see what they'd look like once we reached the penthouse.

"The gambling ends on the sixth floor," he answered. "The top three floors are just bedrooms."

So we made our way up one more flight, and the only difference between the sixth floor of the Central Hotel and the casino at Monte Carlo was that a third of the players here were Chinamen and the girls were all dressed for mighty warm weather.

"See that big Chinaman in the corner with his back to the wall?" whispered Harvey, gesturing to an ornery-looking feller sitting at a high-stakes poker table. "He's Lo Chung. He owns the place." He pointed to the others at the table. "That's Bet-A-Million Reynolds, over there is Sir Reginald Thurmand, and that little guy next to Lo Chung is Gerhardt Guenther, the German ambassador." He sighed. "Must be fifty million dollars sitting at that one table."

"They got a privy up here?" I asked as one of the hostesses passed by, and she pointed it out to me. I told Harvey to stay put, then went off by myself, pulled out a handkerchief, folded it into a nice neat square, folded Cornwall's money over it, and then slapped a rubber band around the whole thing, so it looked like I was walking around with maybe forty thousand pounds of cash rather than four hundred.

Then I went back out onto the floor and rejoined Harvey, who was getting a little nervous in the presence of all that money. We wandered around the room, exchanged pleasantries with a couple of hostesses, stopped to watch the action at the roulette wheel and the craps table, and finally wound up at the fan-tan game, where a Greek and a Korean were having a contest to see who could go broke first. I whispered to Harvey to go back to the rickshaw and that I'd meet him there in just a couple of minutes. He looked kind of curious, but he did what I told him.

"I *do* love the smell of money," I said, turning back to the fan-tan table.

"Perhaps you would like to join us," suggested the Greek.

I shook my head. "Too tame for me, brother."

He laughed so loud that everyone turned to see what was going on.

"You find fan-tan *tame*?" he said.

"Yeah. It's almost as dull as poker and craps," I said. I pulled out my bankroll, tossed it carelessly in the air and caught it a couple of times, and then stuck it back in my pocket. "Guess I'll go out looking for some *real* action."

At which point Lo Chung got up from his poker game and walked over to me.

"Good evening, Father," he said, bowing low.

"As a matter of fact, it's Reverend," I said. "The Right Reverend Lucifer Jones."

"It is not often that we play host to a man of the cloth," he said. "We have a reputation as the Sin City of the Orient."

"Well, I'm afraid it's gonna be even less often, brother," I said. "I like excitement when I bet." I reached into my pocket and fiddled with my bankroll again. "Nothing all that exciting here, except maybe for that little hostess with the green eyes and dress to match."

"We try to accommodate all our guests, Reverend Jones," he said, looking greedily toward my pocket. "Perhaps if you would tell me what type of gambling excites you...?"

"Glad you asked, brother," I said, kind of gently shoving him aside and speaking to the room at large. "Ladies and gents, I came here by rickshaw, just like a batch of you folks did—and I got forty thousand pounds that says my rickshaw puller can whip any rickshaw puller you put up against him at any distance from fifty yards to six furlongs at equal weights."

"Now just a minute, Reverend Jones!" said Lo Chung. "This is *my* gambling establishment. You cannot arrange your own transactions with my customers!"

"Sorry, Brother Lo Chung," I apologized. "I certainly didn't mean to step out of line. I suppose I'd best take my leave of you."

I walked to the head of the stairs, and then stopped and turned back to the room. "The race starts in front of the Macau Inn at nine o'clock tomorrow morning," I said. "I'll cover any and all bets."

Then I ran down the stairs just before a couple of Lo Chung's bouncers could throw me down. I saw the cutest little lady serving drinks as I passed the third floor, but I didn't have time to start no conversations and I figured if I just grabbed her and carried her down the stairs with me the extra weight would slow me down enough so the bouncers could catch me, and so a brief and tender romantic moment went unrequited.

I yelled to Harvey to get ready to roll as I burst out through the front door with a couple of hundred coolies staring at me, but no one followed me, so thankfully he didn't have to use up no energy or calories or nothing getting us out of there, and ten minutes later we were back at the Macau Inn, sitting in the bar, him sipping an iced tea and eyeing my beer the way I had eyed that little hostess on the third floor.

"Have you given any serious thought to how you plan to cover all those bets tomorrow?" he asked.

"Me and the Lord'll think of something," I said. "After all, we got all night, ain't we?"

"All night isn't that long, Preacher."

"The Lord made the world in six days," I said. "That's one for each continent, the way I figure it. Now, if He could make Asia in a day and have time left over for creating the sun and the moon and swiping one of Adam's ribs, surely He don't need all night to solve this minor inconvenience." I finished up my beer. "You just make sure you don't bust no legs coming out of the starting gate."

"I could beat most of the local coolies on one leg," answered Harvey. "Don't worry, Preacher—it's in the bag."

"All right," I said. "It's about time you headed home and got a good eight hours, so you'll be all fresh and ready to go in the morning." Then I changed my mind. "You know, now as I come to think on it, it's probably better that you spend the night here. Can't chance you running into traffic and getting all tuckered out on your way here tomorrow morning."

"I don't have any money for a room."

I tossed him my room key. "Take mine," I said. "I'll get another. You can pay me out of your share of the winnings."

He picked up the key and headed off to the room. Then, just to make sure he didn't do nothing to damage his wind on the eve of the big event, I rounded up all the girls in the lobby, rented another room, and made sure that none of 'em were available just in case he came looking for a little infraction. It was a long and arduous chore, but I figured I owed it to him, and I was sure that my Silent

Partner would understand that I was only doing it for the benefit of His tabernacle.

I got up a bit before sunrise, tiptoed out of the room, and went down to the front desk, where a young Chinaman was smoking a waterpipe and doping out the races.

"Got a safe deposit box for hire, brother?" I asked.

"Yes," said the clerk, pulling out a box and handing me the key. "That'll be one Hong Kong dollar."

"How'd you like to make some *real* money?" I said.

"I wouldn't be averse to it," he admitted.

"Good," I said. "Comes nine o'clock, this place is gonna be crawling with rickshaws and big spenders. A lot of them are going to want someone responsible to hold their bets." I pulled a pair of hundred-pound notes off my roll, which was still wrapped around the handkerchief, and handed them to him. "This ought to make it worth your while."

"Yes, sir!" he said with a great big smile.

"Now, as you can see," I said, sticking the roll into the box, "I'm putting forty thousand pounds in here. You're my witness."

"Right," he said, barely taking his eyes off his own two hundred-pound notes, which was probably close to half a year's wages for him.

"Okay," I said, handing him the box. "Lock it up for safekeeping."

He put the box back in place, locked it, and returned the key to me.

"Now, just so you've got this straight: you're legally empowered to take bets up to forty thousand pounds. Once you've reached the limit, or there ain't no more money being wagered, stick it in another lock box and keep the key yourself."

"Then what?"

"The winner gets the contents of both boxes." I leaned across the counter and whispered in his ear: "And if things go right, this could be a daily chore for you—at the same rate of pay."

"I'm more than happy to be of service, sir," he assured me with a greedy grin on his face.

"Somehow I thought you might be," I replied.

Then I went off to wake Harvey, took him down to the restaurant for a breakfast of orange juice and tea, and walked back into the lobby at about a quarter to nine. It was filled to overflowing with coolies and their backers, all lined up to lay their bets with the clerk.

At nine o'clock sharp, we all walked outside, where Harvey and twenty-three other rickshaw pullers lined up across the broad street. Then it was just a matter of setting the conditions, which turned out to be twice around the block, or just under half a mile. Harvey was pawing at the ground with his feet, and his eyes were bright and excited, and I thought he might break out whinnying any second.

There must have been a good five hundred people crowded up and down the street, not all of them Chinamen, and finally we let Bet-A-Million Reynolds fire the gun that started the race.

Harvey opened up a quick two lengths on his field before they hit the first corner, and was leading by twenty yards when they passed the finish line the first time. They disappeared from sight around the corner a second time, and when they hit the home-stretch Harvey was only leading by a length—but as he passed by he winked at me, and I realized he was just trying not to discourage the competition from trying him again. He won by about half a length, and before I could go to the desk to pick up our winnings, Sir Reginald Thurmand and Ambassador Gerhardt Guenther were demanding a rematch that night.

I hemmed and hawed as if I thought Harvey was too tuckered out to run again, and finally let them talk me into it, for midnight, sharp. We told the crowd when to come back, and then Harvey and me went to the desk and picked up 37,000 beautiful British pounds, counted it a couple of times and stood there admiring it for a few minutes, and then put it back in the safe.

"Easiest money I ever made for a rickshaw ride!" he laughed.

"We should just about double it tonight," I said, "and then we'll start running you in handicaps."

"Handicaps?"

"Yeah," I said. "After this weekend we'll never get another even race, so you'll probably have to tote weights in your rickshaw, just like a racehorse."

"Make the race downhill and the weights might actually help me go faster," he suggested.

"That little law of physics ain't exactly lost on me," I replied. "Ain't no law says you have to run the same course every time out."

Well, we loafed around the hotel for most of the afternoon, but when I saw Harvey smiling at a couple of early-blooming flowers of the night I sent him to his room for a nap, and then, just to make sure that he couldn't give in to temptation, I took them off to my own room for the next couple of hours, where I got me an education in various Chinese arts that were even more complicated than fan-tan.

I could have spent another few hours saving Harvey from further temptation, and generous Christian gentleman that I am I was all set to do so, but at about seven o'clock he pounded on my door to say that he was going down to the restaurant to grab some dinner. I didn't want his stomach to go cramping up on him, so I took my leave of my lovely companions and went with him to supervise.

"I'll have a thick steak, and make sure that it's rare," said Harvey as the waiter approached us.

"Belay that order," I said. "He'll have two glasses of orange juice and a cup of coffee."

"Preacher," he said irritably, "sooner or later you got to let me eat something solid or I ain't gonna have the energy to run. I'm starving!"

"You can't run on a full stomach," I told him sternly.

"I can't run on one that's been empty for a day and a half, neither!"

"You're really all that hungry?" I asked.

"I am."

"Okay," I said, turning to the waiter. "Bring us a thick steak."

"Rare," added Harvey.

"Yes, sir," said the waiter, bowing.

"Does that come with a salad?" I asked.

"Yes, sir."

"Fine. Bring 'em out at the same time."

"And what will you have, sir?"

"I'm having the steak. My friend here gets the salad. No dressing."

"Preacher!"

"Ah, what the hell," I said, giving in to my soft Christian nature. "Bring him a half order of dressing, on the side."

"Thanks a heap," muttered Harvey.

He didn't say another word till the salad came, and then he wolfed it down so fast I thought he might take a couple of bites out of the plate by mistake, or maybe on purpose, and I noticed that he licked my steak plate clean while I was settling the bill, but when we left the restaurant I was satisfied that he was in perfect shape for the race.

The crowds started showing up at about ten o'clock, and by a quarter to midnight there must have been a thousand people, but the betting was going real slow since Harvey had impressed the hell out of 'em in the morning and they wanted to wait to see the opposition and have the odds posted before they started laying their money down.

Then, suddenly, everything got real quiet, and a big black limousine pulled up and Lo Chung stepped out. He looked like he'd had happier days.

"Howdy, Lo Chung," I said, stepping forward. "Welcome to the Sin City Rickshaw Racing Club. I thought you'd be tending to business over at the Central Hotel."

"All my customers have come *here*," he said grimly.

"Well, we'll shoot 'em right back to you once the race is over."

"You must not continue to interfere with my business, Reverend Jones," he said.

"Who's interfering?" I said. "You run roulette wheels and fan-tan games, I run rickshaw races."

"I warn you, Reverend. I am becoming seriously displeased with you."

"Six or seven weeks, and everyone'll get tired of trying to beat my champion and go back to blowing their paychecks over at your place, Lo Chung," I said. "You just gotta learn to be patient."

"Just remember, Doctor Jones, that my patience is not unending," he said, and got back into his limo and drove off to the Central Hotel.

Well, that kind of put a damper on things for a couple of minutes, but then Sir Reginald and the German ambassador showed up, each with what looked like a higher class of coolie, and a few minutes later the race was underway, and this time the coolies broke on top and Harvey just kind of lagged behind in third place, biding his time until the last hundred yards or so, where he came on to win by just under a length.

We cleared another twenty thousand pounds, stuck it with the rest of our money in the hotel safe, and went to bed, him alone and me with such temptations as I didn't want him to have no part of.

Next morning I woke him up again, and escorted him down to the restaurant.

"You know what I dreamed about last night?" he said after I'd ordered him a grapefruit juice and a cup of coffee.

"Women?" I suggested.

"Nope."

"America?"

He shook his head. "Food."

"Harvey, I'm your manager," I said. "You gotta trust me. Haven't I made us close to 60,000 pounds already?"

"Sooner or later you gotta give me something to eat or I'm gonna be too weak to pull that damned rickshaw," he protested.

"After this morning's race," I said. "We'll give you an hour to cool out, and then you can have the biggest steak on the menu. That'll give you more than twelve hours to digest it and sleep it off before you run again at midnight."

"You promise?" he asked distrustfully.

"I swear it on my mother's grave," I said, which seemed to please him. At any rate, it had to have pleased him more than knowing that my mother was currently running an establishment for fallen women in Wichita, which was in fact the case, but somehow it just wouldn't have sounded as impressive to swear on my mother's sporting house.

Well, we finished breakfast and walked outside, shouldering our way through a few hundred Chinamen, and what we came to was Lo Chung, leaning against his limousine and doing his damnedest to look inscrutable.

"You're up early today, Lo Chung," I said by way of greeting.

"I finally decided that if I couldn't beat you, I should join you," he replied.

"Well, that's right thoughtful of you," I said, "but the Sin City Jockey Club ain't in the market for no partners."

"I meant that I intend to join you as a competitor," he explained. "Let me make sure I have the conditions correct. You state that your man can outpull any rickshaw in Macau?"

"That's right."

"And there are no other conditions?"

I shot a quick look at Harvey, figuring that Lo Chung was thinking of bringing in some Chinese track star who we hadn't never heard of, but he just gave me a confident nod.

"That's right," I said. "There's ain't no other conditions."

He pulled a huge wad of bills out of his pocket. "I'll match whatever winnings you've accrued so far."

I looked at Harvey again. He looked fit and trim and confident, even if his stomach *was* rumbling to beat the band.

"Okay, Lo Chung, you got yourself a bet," I said, and escorted him to the desk while he placed his roll on deposit in the safe.

"Shall we outline the course?" he asked as we were walking back to the street.

"Well, usually they just run around the block a couple of times," I said.

"This may be the biggest wager ever made on a race in Macau," he answered. "I think more people should be able to see it. I suggest that we race from the ruins of the St. Paul Cathedral to the Temple of Kun Iam."

"That's pretty close to a mile," I noted.

"Isn't your man up to it?" he asked with a smile.

"Five yards, five miles, it makes no difference to me," said Harvey.

"Excellent!" said Lo Chung. "Shall we walk to the starting line?"

"Wouldn't you rather wait by the finish?" I asked.

"All in good time, Reverend Jones," he said. "I'll see the finish, too, never fear."

I figured that meant he planned to have his limo drive him to the finish line once the race was underway, and made up my mind to hop a lift with him since I didn't relish walking all the way to the Temple of Kun Iam in the morning sun.

The St. Paul Cathedral, which had fallen into a mild state of disrepair and now consisted of nothing but four walls, a staircase, and a lot of weeds, was about half a mile from the Macau Inn. Harvey, surrounded by a bunch of kids who all wanted his autograph, started toting the rickshaw there, with me and Lo Chung and a few hundred betters tagging along behind. As we were walking I realized that I'd been so busy watching Harvey's diet that I'd neglected to eat breakfast myself, so I stopped by a local food stand and bought a couple of sandwiches and an apple, stuffed the apple and one of the sandwiches in my pocket, and munched on the other as we made our way to the starting line.

"By the way, I ain't seen *your* rickshaw yet, Brother Lo Chung," I said.

"It's waiting for us at the Cathedral."

When we got to within maybe fifty yards of the Cathedral, I turned to him. "You must be wrong, Brother Lo Chung," I said. "Ain't nothing there but a horse and buggy."

"A horse and *rickshaw*," he corrected me.

"Well, that's one way of getting it here," I said. "Where's your puller?"

"Right there, Reverend Jones," he replied.

"But that's a horse!"

"How clever of you to notice."

"That ain't in the rules! Get rid of it and get yourself a man to pull your rickshaw!"

"You explicitly stated that your man could outpull any rickshaw on Macau," said Lo Chung. "You never said that it had to be pulled by another man. *That* is my puller."

"No way!" I yelled. "You get a man in front of that rickshaw or the bet's off!"

"The bet is *on*, Reverend Jones," he said, and suddenly I was looking down the barrels of a couple of dozen pistols in the hands of his friends and relations, all of who were dressed in black. "Perhaps next time you will think more carefully before cutting in on someone else's business."

"Well, maybe I'll just tie *our* rickshaw onto the back of a car," I said.

"That would be against the rules," said Lo Chung. "You've already named your puller. He's the one taking on all challengers, remember?"

"I'm gonna have to think about this," I said.

"Well, think quickly," said Lo Chung. "The race starts in seven minutes."

I walked over to Harvey.

"What about it?" I asked in low tones. "Think you can beat a horse?"

"Not a chance," he said dejectedly.

Then an interesting notion struck me. "Don't be so all-fired sure of that," I told him. "The horse don't know he's in a race, does he?"

"What are you driving at, Preacher?" asked Harvey.

"When the race starts, why don't you just walk calm and natural-like toward the Temple of Kun Iam? If he ain't got no reason to run, he'll either stay right where he is or fall into step behind you. Maybe we can win this thing without you breaking out of a walk!"

"I think you've got something there, Preacher!" he said excitedly. "Let's give it a try!"

"Okay, Lo Chung," I said, walking back to the Chinaman. "We accept your puller."

"Good," he said, walking over to his rickshaw. "I knew you'd see the light of reason."

He began clambering up onto the seat.

"*Now* what the hell are you doing?" I demanded.

"I'm willingly giving my puller a handicap of 183 pounds," he said.

"You can't do that!"

"There is nothing in the rules prohibiting me from sitting in my rickshaw during the race," he said, as one of his henchmen handed him a whip and another began putting a bridle over the horse's head.

"I *made* the rules!" I shouted. "And I say that ain't legal!"

"Shall we put it to a vote?" asked Lo Chung.

"All right," I said furiously. "Let's just do that!"

Lo Chung nodded to his men, who turned their pistols on the crowd. "Will any man who thinks my actions constitute a breach of the rules please fall down with a bullet in his chest?" he said in a loud, clear voice.

Nobody fell down, or did much of anything else.

He smiled at me. "There you have it, Reverend. A unanimous vote. Now, if you have no further objections, I'll send some of my men ahead to make sure no one absconds with the money."

I had plenty of objections, but it didn't seem all that desirable to voice them at that particular moment. I suggested to my Silent Partner that time was running out fast, and that if He was going to intervene He'd better do it quick, and damned if He didn't come up with an idea.

I looked around until I found an old coolie with a bamboo fishing pole maybe ten or twelve feet long and asked if I could borrow it. I don't think he understood a word I said, but he just kept chattering and bowing until finally I took it out of his hands.

"Going fishing, Reverend?" asked Lo Chung with a chuckle. "I thought you were here to watch a rickshaw race."

"*You* got a whip," I said. "It's only fair that *I* should have a whip."

And with that, I climbed into the chair of Harvey's rickshaw.

"Are you crazy, Preacher?" he demanded. "I can't beat the damned horse *without* you!"

"Fair is fair," I said, smiling back at Lo Chung. "And when we win, I don't ever want anyone saying we done it because Harvey didn't have a passenger and the horse did."

Lo Chung busted out laughing at that, and Harvey kept muttering to himself, and a couple of minutes later we were lined up, nose to nose, in front of St. Paul's Cathedral, pointing toward the Temple of Kun Iam about a mile away.

"Are the contestants ready?" asked Sir Reginald, who had volunteered to be the official starter.

"Not quite," I said, fiddling with the wire on the end of the fishing pole.

"What are you doing, Reverend Jones?" demanded Lo Chung suspiciously.

"Just making sure my whip is in working order," I said.

"You whip me with that thing and I'll give you the beating of your life!" muttered Harvey under his breath.

"Okay, now I'm ready," I said after another moment or two.

"Splendid!" said Sir Reginald. He pulled out his little ivory-handled revolver. "On your marks, get set, go!"

He shot the pistol off just as I swung the fishing pole, with my apple attached to it, in front of the horse's face. He lunged at it, almost throwing Lo Chung out of the rickshaw, and Harvey got off to a quick lead.

"What's going on back there, Preacher?" he asked as he ran along. "Where the hell is the horse?"

"You worry about the running, and leave the horse to me," I said, hanging over the side and dangling the apple just in front of the horse's nose. Whenever he reached for it, I flicked my hand and moved it a few inches away from him.

Lo Chung was beating the horse with his whip and cussing a blue streak, but evidently the poor animal hadn't had no more to eat than Harvey had, because he just ignored Lo Chung and kept his eyes peeled on the apple.

Well, we ambled along like that for almost three quarters of a mile, and I took a quick peek ahead and could see the Temple of Kun Iam maybe three hundred yards ahead of us. Then our rickshaw hit a big dip in the road and I almost fell out, and by the time I had regained my balance the horse had reached out and finally got his teeth into the apple and bit it off.

"Step it up, Harvey!" I yelled. "We got problems!"

The horse didn't speed up, but he didn't slow down none either, and I could see that he was going to be done with the apple before we crossed the finish line, and there wasn't no doubt in my mind that once that particular event came to pass he would finally respond to the whip that Lo Chung kept beating him with.

Then I remembered the other sandwich that I had tucked away in my pocket, and I figured what worked for one puller might work for another, so I quick tied it to the end of the fishing rod just about the time the horse downed the last of the apple and we had maybe forty yards to go.

I reached out and stuck it just out of Harvey's reach, and he took off with a burst of speed that would have done Jim Thorpe proud. Lo Chung's rickshaw was coming up fast on the left, but Harvey was inspired, and we crossed the finish line a good half-length in front.

I let Harvey grab the sandwich then, and he kept running as he stuffed it in his mouth.

"You can stop now!" I said. "We won!"

"I saw fifteen of Lo Chung's friends and relations standing there in front of the Temple with their guns out and looking very upset for this early in the day," he hollered back at me.

"But we got all our money back at the Macau Inn!" I said.

"It's only money."

"What's so *only* about money?" I demanded.

"You do what you gotta do, Preacher," said Harvey, heading straight toward the dock. "Me, I'm getting out of town alive and intact. There'll be other rickshaw races, and I aim to have my legs still attached to the rest of me when I run in 'em."

I looked back and saw Lo Chung standing beside his rickshaw, raising all kinds of a ruckus, and then a few of his friends and relations looked after us and fired a couple of shots in our direction, and suddenly a boat trip to the mainland started looking better and better.

"After all," I said aloud, "what is a man profited if he wins a hundred thousand pounds sterling and loses his innerds?"

Harvey said "Amen!" and jacked up the pace as the Temple of Kun Iam faded into the distance behind us.

3. THE INSIDIOUS ORIENTAL DENTIST

Once we hit the mainland, Harvey and I parted company. He wanted to get right back into the rickshaw-racing business, but I decided to head off to Peking, which was the capital city of China and figured to have not only the most sinners in need of saving but the most opportunities to raise funds for my tabernacle.

Well, let me tell you something: it ain't no short hop from Macau to Peking. It took me six months to get there, during which time I picked up a smattering of the language, fell in love fourteen or fifteen times, and only got a personal tour of one calaboose. That was in a little town called Poshan, where the apple of my eye turned out to be the fruit of the local warlord's loins, but even that worked out for the good, because I lost a quick ten pounds on the prison grub and was more handsome than ever by the time I got the jailkeeper interested in a little game of chance involving the number twenty-one, and won my freedom.

By the time I finally got within hailing distance of Peking I wasn't looking my very best, not having changed clothes for the better part of half a year, and despite taking a plunge into any river I passed by I wasn't on the verge of turning into any nosegay neither, so I started scouting around the countryside for some of the Christian missions I'd heard had been built in these parts. It didn't take too long to find one, where I stopped in for a meal and a little discussion of the Good Book—I'm kind of weak on the Sermon on the Mount, but I'll match my knowledge of the why and how of all the begattings with the best of 'em—and on the way out I borrowed a new set of missionary clothes that I found drying on a clothesline, since I knew these fellers wouldn't begrudge them to a fellow Christian, and besides, I figured an act of inadvertent charity would put them in real tight with the Lord, Who appreciates such things if not done to excess.

I was still some fifty miles out of Peking when I managed to land a ride in the back of a truck that was hauling bales of hay into the city. It was getting on toward winter, and I didn't have no overcoat, so I just kind of burrowed into the hay and decided to catch a quick thirty or forty winks.

I was awakened by a tall, thin Englishman jabbing me with his cane.

"You!" he said. "Get out of there, and be quick about it!"

I sat up, rubbed my eyes, and saw that he was pointing a revolver at my middle, which got my attention right fast.

"What were you doing in there?" he demanded, and as I climbed out I saw that he had the driver out of the cab, too.

"Mostly, I was being woke up by an Englishman with a gun," I said. "If this is a holdup, brother, I got to inform you that I'm a man of the cloth who's taken a temporary vow of poverty. I ain't got nothing to my name but the clothes on my back and my copy of the Good Book."

He turned to the driver and jabbered something in Chinese so quick that I couldn't follow what he was saying. The driver, who looked scared to death, nodded his head and grunted.

"All right," said the Englishman. "You can go."

"Go *where*?" I said. "I don't even know where I am."

The driver said something else, and this time it was the Englishman who nodded and grunted, and a minute later the driver hopped back into the cab and took off.

"*Now* how am I gonna get into the city?" I said.

"I'll drive you," said the Englishman. "Where are you going?"

"Peking."

"I mean, where in Peking?"

"I ain't figured that out yet," I said. "Just getting here was effort enough."

He peered at me intently. "You've never been here before?"

"As God is my witness."

He kept on staring at me. "And you're really a man of the cloth?"

I held up two fingers and pressed them together. "Me and God are just like *that*," I assured him.

"Excellent!" He walked me over to his jeep, which we both got into. "What's your name?" he asked, as we headed off toward Peking.

"The Honorable Right Reverend Doctor Lucifer Jones, at your service. Baptisms and funerals done cheap."

"How would you like the opportunity to help me defeat Satan Incarnate, Reverend Jones?" he asked.

"Satan Incarnate?" I repeated.

He nodded his head vigorously.

"He lives in Peking, does he?" I said.

"Peking is his headquarters, but he has residences all over the world."

"How many residences?"

He shrugged. "Fifteen, twenty, who can say?"

Which made the odds fifteen or twenty to one that he wouldn't be at home today, and I got to thinking that maybe I could appropriate a few Satanic artifacts for the local pawn shop.

"Sure," I said. "Standing up to Satan is one of the very best things I do, me being a man of God and all."

"Excellent!" said the Englishman. "It's been a long, lonely battle. But with you on our side, we just might win." He paused for a minute. "Allow me to introduce myself. I am Sir Mortimer Edgerton-Smythe."

"Pleased to meet you," I said. "Who else is on our side?"

"There's just you and me," he said.

"And how many are in the opposition?"

"Who can say? Surely thousands, possibly hundreds of thousands. Perhaps millions. Have you ever heard of Doctor Aristotle Ho?"

"Can't say that I have."

"He is the fiend who heads this secret organization," said Sir Mortimer, his eyes blazing with hatred. "His father was a Grecian ambassador, his mother the daughter of a Chinese warlord. Nothing is known of his childhood. We *do* know that he spent three years practicing dentistry in Hangchou before he began his nefarious career by taking over the leadership of the local tong. From there he spread out, assimilating one criminal organization after another, until today he is the most powerful villain on the continent. His tentacles are everywhere, Reverend Jones. They reach not only into Peking, but to the capitals of Europe itself. He dreams of worldwide conquest, and he is more than halfway to his goal, and yet so careful has he been, so circumspect, that almost no one has ever heard of him."

"You've met this Doctor Aristotle Ho?" I asked.

"Twice," said Sir Mortimer. "The first time was in England, where I prevented him from stealing the Crown jewels. The second time was in Chunking, where I barely escaped with my life."

"I assume you're working for the British government?"

"That's correct."

"Why don't you guys just march in an army or two and blow him away?" I asked.

"We're operating in a foreign land, Reverend Jones," he said. "We can't just send our troops in and destroy him. Our only hope is to prove that he is guilty of breaking international law, and then arrest him."

"And how do you plan to do that?" I asked.

"The dragon is the key to it."

"Dragon?"

"Doctor Ho keeps an enormous dragon on his estate," began Sir Mortimer.

"There ain't no such things," I said. "They're just imaginary beasts, like dinosaurs and unicorns and honest redheads named Bernice."

"That's what I thought, too, until I saw it with my own eyes," said Sir Mortimer. "But it exists, and it's the way we shall bring him down."

"You plan to feed him to this here dragon?" I asked curiously.

He shook his head. "No," he said. "Britain is a nation of laws. I intend to use the law to put an end to his villainy."

"How is a dragon gonna help you do that?" I asked. "I thought they didn't do much except eat knights and virgins and things like that."

"This dragon eats just about anything that moves," answered Sir Mortimer. "The truck in which you were riding belongs to Doctor Ho; it was carrying hay and grain to fatten the cattle he feeds to the dragon. That's why I inspected it; I wanted to see if he was smuggling anything else into his fortress."

"You still ain't told me how the dragon is gonna cause Doctor Ho's downfall," I said.

"I'm coming to that," said Sir Mortimer. "Every year Doctor Ho ships the dragon to a different city for the Chinese New Year festival: Hong Kong, Shanghai, once even San Francisco. The dragon remains for a week, and is then shipped back. Last year he shipped it to Rio de Janeiro."

"So?"

"Reverend Jones," he said triumphantly, "*there are only seventeen Chinese in Rio de Janeiro—and eleven of them don't even celebrate the New Year!* The man is obviously smuggling something, and if we can just find out what it is, we can put him behind bars for life!"

"When's the next Chinese New Year coming up?" I asked.

"Soon! The dragon is due to be shipped out tomorrow."

"Exactly what do you think he's smuggling, Sir Mortimer?" I asked.

"That remains to be discovered."

"And just how do we plan to discover it?"

"Tonight, after dark, we'll sneak into the dragon's enclosure and examine both the beast and its cage. If there's any contraband there, from drugs to jewels, we'll find it—and that will be the undoing of the insidious Aristotle Ho!"

The only reason I didn't hop out of the car right then and there was because I didn't believe in dragons. I figured Sir Mortimer was like so many other Englishmen I'd met, who had a passion for foreign lands but never remembered to properly protect his head from the vertical rays of the sun, and was now just a bit on the dotty side.

So you can imagine my surprise when we drove out to this huge estate after dark, and the first thing I heard was a roar that was like unto a volcano erupting.

"Good!" whispered Sir Mortimer. "We're in time! They haven't shipped him off yet!"

I opened the door. "Well, Sir Mortimer," I said, "it sure has been nice knowing you, and if you ever need spiritual comforting, why, you just be sure to look me up."

I started walking back in the general direction of Peking, but he ran around the car and grabbed me.

"Just where do you think you're going?" he demanded.

"Where's the dragon?" I asked.

"Right over there," he said, pointing to the left.

"Good," I said, heading off to the right. "I'm going *this* way."

"I need your help, damn it!"

"You need a short list of funeral prayers for crazy Englishmen," I said. "Little yellow guys who want to take over the world don't bother me none, but I ain't going into no corral with no dragon."

"I thought you were sworn to combat evil wherever you found it."

"I didn't swear to go hunting it up when it's peacefully minding its own business in its pasture."

"My people have posted a million-pound reward to the man who brings Doctor Ho to justice," he said desperately. "I'll split it down the middle with you!"

Which put a whole new light on things.

"Well, my tabernacle *does* need a new altar," I admitted, "along with walls and floors and pews and a steeple and a ceiling. You got yourself a deal, Sir Mortimer."

"Good! Let's get busy."

He led me over to a huge paddock with a high fence around it.

"He's inside, in the barn," whispered Sir Mortimer.

"How do you know?" I asked, kind of nervous-like.

"If he was outside, he'd have heard us by now, and would be roaring and spouting flames that would illuminate the whole area."

"Just how big is this here dragon?" I asked.

"Perhaps half a city block."

I was about to ask if that was a long New York block or a short Macau block when it suddenly occurred to me that it didn't really make an awful lot of difference, given the current situation.

Sir Mortimer led me around the paddock to a broad driveway that led to an oversized barn.

"You're *sure* this is the only way to get the goods on Aristotle Ho?" I asked as he reached out for the door.

"Just don't make any sudden movements," he said.

"Uh…I don't wanna sound like I lack confidence in this here operation, Sir Mortimer—but have you ever searched a dragon before?"

"As a matter of fact, I've searched this dragon four previous times," answered Sir Mortimer. "Each of the past four years, just before he's shipped out, I've gone over him with a fine-toothed comb. I've checked his harness for jewels, I've gone over every inch of his cage, I've even gone through his stool in case Doctor Ho is trying to ship some contraband *inside* him."

"And you ain't never found nothing?"

"Never," he admitted.

"Then why bother doing it all over again tonight?" I asked.

"Because I'm convinced that the answer lies with the dragon." He frowned resolutely. "I'll just have to be more thorough this time."

The building shook with another roar.

"If you've done this before, you don't really need *me*," I suggested.

"Oh, I've always had help," he said.

"Yeah?"

He nodded. "Poor chaps."

He opened the door and pulled me inside before I had a chance to ask what happened to them. Given the sight that met my eyes, that was probably all for the best.

There was just one stall in the barn. It was made of steel bars, and it was maybe 200 feet long and 100 feet wide, and while it was filled with straw and food troughs and water drums, what it was mostly filled with was a dragon. He was green on top, bright yellow on the bottom, and scaly all over. The second I looked at him I decided he was big enough to eat a couple of dinosaurs for lunch and still be ready to polish off the Eiffel Tower or some similar tidbit for dinner. He had the longest, ugliest face I ever did see, with big red eyes the size of basketballs, and a nose that kept snorting smoke.

"Good evening, Cuddles," said Sir Mortimer gently.

"*Cuddles?*" I repeated.

"It's my pet name for him," said Sir Mortimer. "It makes him seem less formidable."

Cuddles roared again, and a flame a dozen feet long shot out of his mouth and barely missed us.

"They really shouldn't keep him on straw bedding," noted Sir Mortimer. "He's likely to set the place on fire." He paused. "Hmm... I suppose if we don't find the contraband, I could always report Doctor Ho to the local branch of the S.P.C.A."

"How in the world do they ship something like this?" I asked.

Sir Mortimer pointed to a number of barred cage sections piled up against the wall. "There's his traveling cage," he said. "They'll assemble it tomorrow morning and then drive him into it." He sighed deeply. "Well, I daresay we'd best get to work."

"Couldn't we just kind of examine him from right here?" I asked, positioning myself directly behind Sir Mortimer.

"No," he said. "If the contraband could be spotted from outside his cage, it *would* have been."

"What makes you so sure there *is* any contraband?" I asked.

"There *has* to be," answered Sir Mortimer firmly. "It's the only way Doctor Ho can finance his far-flung enterprises. I know all his other sources of income, and they simply don't amount to enough. No, Reverend Jones, it's *got* to be here!"

And with that, he opened the door to the stall, and, taking me by the arm, pulled me inside.

"I'll check out his feet," said Sir Mortimer, pulling out a flashlight. "You'd be surprised what can be hidden inside nails this size."

"What do I do?" I asked nervously, as the dragon turned his head to face me.

"He's wearing a halter on his head," said Sir Mortimer. "Make sure there are no jewels attached to it."

"I can't see none."

"Check the underside of the leather."

"You're kidding, right?"

"I'm perfectly serious."

I took another look at the dragon, which looked like it was just itching for a little snack of charred missionary.

"You *got* to be kidding!" I insisted. "You don't expect me to—"

At that instant the dragon roared again, and I just barely ducked the flames that shot out at me.

"Ah! I see they've chemically treated the straw so it can't catch fire," said Sir Mortimer. "Too bad. So much for the S.P.C.A."

He went back to examining the dragon's toenails, and I took a tentative step toward the dragon's face.

"Nice Cuddles," I said. "Cute Cuddles."

Cuddles glared at me and growled. No fire came out, but I damned near choked to death on the smoke.

"Sweet Cuddles," I said, taking a couple of more steps that brought me right beneath his face.

"Careful now," said Sir Mortimer, pulling a hammer and an icepick out of his pocket. "This may hurt."

He stuck the icepick up against one of the dragon's toenails and banged on it. Cuddles let out another roar that could be heard all the way to Sioux City.

"Damn it, Sir Mortimer!" I yelled.

"Sorry. Just being thorough."

I turned back to Cuddles, who was still staring at me.

"Now, just take it easy feller," I said. "I just want to look at your harness."

I reached up to let him smell the back of my hand, like you're supposed to do with dogs and such. He took a sniff and practically inhaled my whole arm.

"Sir Mortimer!" I hollered.

"Quiet, or you'll wake the whole fortress!" hissed Sir Mortimer.

"But my arm's stuck in his nose, and he won't give it back!"

Sir Mortimer nodded his head sadly, without looking up from the dragon's toenails. "Yes, that happened to poor Archie, too."

"Who was poor Archie?" I asked, trying to pull my arm loose.

"The assistant I lost on my second—or was it my third? No, definitely my second—inspection of the dragon."

I looked up at Cuddles, who was staring at me with a kind of stupid expression on his face.

"Okay," I said. "Fun's fun. Now leggo of my arm."

Cuddles just kept looking at me and not doing much of anything, and it occurred to me that dragons maybe didn't breathe more than once every ten or twenty minutes.

"Sir Mortimer, I really could use a little help here!" I said.

"Not now, Reverend."

I yanked once or twice more, to no effect. Then I started twitching my fingers, just to make sure they were still attached, and suddenly Cuddles let out with a sneeze that blew me halfway across the stall.

"Stop clowning around," said Sir Mortimer, taking a look at me as I rolled to a stop. "This is serious business."

Right at that second I would have been hard pressed to tell you which of them I hated more, Cuddles or Sir Mortimer, but I think Sir Mortimer was in the lead. In fact, the only reason I approached the dragon's head again was because I knew Sir Mortimer wasn't going to let me out of that barn until we'd finished our search.

This time I knew better than to stick out my hand. In fact, the more I studied old Cuddles, the more I got to wondering how *anyone* approached him, and that led to my wondering how they got him into and out of the barn and into his cage, and that led me to think that someone had to have trained him to obey some simple commands. So I looked him right in his red eyes and said, in the sternest voice I could muster under the circumstances, "Sit!"

And damned if he didn't sit right down on his haunches.

"What did you do, Reverend?" asked Sir Mortimer, running to my side.

"I got a way with dumb animals," I explained to Sir Mortimer. "Now stand back and give him room. Down, Cuddles!"

Cuddles collapsed in a heap.

"Amazing!" said Sir Mortimer.

I started going over the harness, while Sir Mortimer examined whatever it was he was examining, but we had to admit after another ten minutes that there wasn't nothing hidden on Cuddles.

"I think I'd best examine his bedding next," said Sir Mortimer. "Do you think he'll be willing to follow you outside?"

"I can't see no reason why not," I said, sliding open the door to his pasture. "Come, Cuddles."

Cuddles almost trampled Sir Mortimer as he got to his feet and bounded out into the pasture behind me. He was feeling right frisky, and he galloped once or twice around it before I noticed that he was starting to spout a little fire and I told him to stop. Then I saw a couple of lights go on in the fortress up on the hill overlooking the pasture, which didn't bode no good, and I figured that if I was gonna get in any kind of a set-to with Doctor Aristotle Ho and his friends that the safest thing to have on my side was a dragon, so I told Cuddles to stand still, and then I ran to his south end and climbed all the way up his tail and back until I was sitting on top of his neck.

That made me feel a mite safer, even though he didn't smell none too good, and I waited for Sir Mortimer to finish going through the bedding and come out, but when he finally showed up he did so in the company of three or four mean-looking Chinamen who were pointing guns at him, and following them was a thin Chinaman with two-inch fingernails and a droopy mustache dressed all in black satin pajamas.

"Good evening, Reverend Jones," said the thin Chinaman.

"I don't know who you are, brother," I said, "but if you take one more step toward me I'm turning this here dragon loose on you!"

For some reason that seemed to strike his funnybone, because he kind of chuckled and didn't back off so much as a step.

"I am Doctor Aristotle Ho," he said, "and that is *my* dragon. I raised him from an infant, and he would no more attack me than the sun and moon would veer from their heavenly courses."

He uttered a couple of terse commands in Chinese, and Cuddles kneeled down and stretched out his neck flat on the ground. There didn't seem much point to staying on him when he was like that, so I climbed off. Doctor Ho said something else, and Cuddles got up and meekly went back into his stall.

Now the insidious Oriental dentist turned to Sir Mortimer with an amused smile on his face.

"Trespassing, breaking and entering, stealing dragons," he counted off. "What am I to do with you, Sir Mortimer?"

Sir Mortimer gave him a stiff upper British lip and didn't say a word.

"And *you*," he said, turning to me. "Why should you be conspiring against me, Lucifer Jones? What harm have I ever done to you?"

"How'd you know my name?" I asked.

"I know all about you," he replied. "Since the moment Sir Mortimer picked you up, I have had my mignons tracing your every movement for the past five years. I know about your misadventures in Cairo and Johannesburg, about your arrests in Nairobi and Dar-es-Salaam and Mozambique, about your ivory poaching and slave trading, about the mutiny you led aboard a ship on the West Coast of Africa, about your being banished from the continent forever…"

"A series of misunderstandings," I said. "Nothing more."

"About your theft of the Empire Emerald in Hong Kong," he continued, unperturbed. "I even know that Lo Chung has put a price on your head."

"He has?"

"And now here you are, invading my property, even riding my dragon. Frankly, Reverend Jones, I suspect that you are something less than a credit to your church."

"Let me tell you, one doctor to another, that I ain't never done nothing to be ashamed of," I said heatedly. "And if you got a couple of hours and maybe a cold drink with just enough alcohol to pound the germs into submission, I'll be happy to explain my side of all them incidents you just recited."

"Your explanation couldn't interest me less," said Doctor Aristotle Ho. "In fact, under other circumstances I could have used a man of your peculiar abilities on my payroll."

"Well, truth to tell, the facts didn't run all *that* far amuck," I said quickly. "What kind of job did you have in mind?"

"Reverend Jones!" said Sir Mortimer sternly. "You are speaking to the most insidious villain in this part of the world!"

"I got nothing but your word for that, Sir Mortimer," I pointed out. "All I know about this here gentleman is that he treats his animals well and he probably ain't on speaking terms with the local manicurist."

"You interest me, Reverend Jones," said Aristotle Ho.

"Are you going to believe that foul demon, or are you going to believe *me*?" demanded Sir Mortimer. "I tell you, Doctor Ho is planning the conquest of the entire world!"

Doctor Ho turned and stared at Sir Mortimer for a minute. "More groundless accusations, Sir Mortimer?" he said.

"Microdots!" shouted Sir Mortimer suddenly. "That's it! He's hidden microdots on the dragon's scales!"

Doctor Ho shook his head sadly. "Poor deluded man."

"That's got to be the answer!" persisted Sir Mortimer. "We've searched everywhere else. Somewhere on that dragon's skin are some microdots that Doctor Ho is selling to our enemies in Europe. Probably the position of the Pacific Fleet!"

"If I let you examine every inch of my dragon, will that finally satisfy you, Sir Mortimer?" asked Doctor Ho.

"You haven't got the nerve!" said Sir Mortimer. "You know I'll find what I'm looking for!"

Doctor Ho turned to his men. "Make Sir Mortimer comfortable for the night, and when we ship the dragon tomorrow morning, make sure that Sir Mortimer accompanies him." He walked over to Sir Mortimer. "It will take approximately seven weeks for the dragon to reach its destination. You will be given free access to him all the way there and all the way back."

His men started dragging Sir Mortimer off.

"Well, that rids me of *his* unpleasant presence for the next few months," said Dr. Ho, as he began walking back to his fortress.

"Hey!" I said. "What about *me*?"

"What *about* you?" asked Doctor Ho.

"I thought we were gonna talk a little business," I said.

"I don't believe we shall," said Doctor Ho.

"Why the hell not?" I demanded. "I took your side, didn't I?"

"The alternative would have been a swift and painful death."

"What's that got to do with anything?"

"Reverend Jones," he said, "you are perhaps the only man of my acquaintance with even less regard for the laws and morals of society than I myself possess. While I do not necessarily consider that a failing, it does make it difficult for me to trust you."

"Well, as I see it, Doctor Ho, you got two choices," I told him. "You can take me on as a partner, or have me as an enemy. Now, if we was to become partners and you really do take over the world, you could give me a little chunk of it, like say, Australia, and we could plunder it six ways to Sunday and split the take right down the middle. If, on the other hand, you decide you'd rather have me as an enemy, you're not only taking on me but the Lord as well, and take my word for it, the Lord can whip you in straight falls without working up much of a sweat."

"There is a third alternative, you know," he said.

"Yeah? What is that?"

He pulled out a little pearl-handled revolver. "I can kill you right here and now."

Which, in my eagerness for gainful employment, was an alternative I had plumb forgotten to take into account.

"You look pale, Reverend Jones," said Doctor Ho. "And your knees are starting to shake. I fear you must be coming down with fever."

"Well, maybe I'll just mosey back into Peking and lie down for a week or two," I suggested hopefully.

He nodded. "It would be best." He reached out a bony hand and took mine in it. "Let us part friends, Reverend Jones."

"That suits me more and more as I come to think on it," I said sincerely.

"I am glad to have had this little chat with you," he continued. "You are a most interesting man. I have the distinct feeling that our paths will cross again."

"You do?"

"Yes. And next time the outcome may not be so pleasant."

"You still plan to conquer the world?"

"That is a very indiscreet question, Reverend Jones," he said. "Let me answer it this way: whatever my plans may be, Sir Mortimer will never thwart them again."

"You mean there ain't nothing hidden on the dragon or in his cage?" I said.

"That is correct."

"Then how come Sir Mortimer is dead convinced that you're smuggling something out every time you ship the dragon?"

"Sir Mortimer is right," said Doctor Ho with a smile. "The poor fool cannot see the forest for the trees."

"Doctor Ho," I said. "Whatever happens in the future, we're parting friends tonight. Just between you and me and the gatepost, no friend would keep another friend sleepless for days wondering what the hell he was shipping out in that cage."

He looked me up and down for a couple of minutes, and then shrugged.

"All right, Reverend Jones," said Doctor Ho. "This is the very last time I shall need this ploy, so your knowledge will never be able to be used against me. I will tell you the secret because it amuses me to do so, and because only a mind like yours can fully appreciate the subtlety of it." He paused. "Sir Mortimer will spend every day for the next seven weeks searching the dragon, the straw, the food, and the water for these imaginary microdots and non-existent jewels and drugs. He will never find what he is looking for, and he will never prevent me from receiving the money I need to continue my operations—and yet, hundreds of times each day, he will be in physical contact with that which he seeks."

"I don't think I follow you," I said.

"The *cage*, Reverend Jones!" he said with a laugh. "The bars are made of pure platinum. For five years Sir Mortimer has microscopically examined everything within the cage, and has never thought to examine the cage itself."

"Well, I'll be damned!" I said.

"That is a foregone conclusion." Doctor Ho took me by the arm. "Now that you know, I'm afraid you must remain as my guest for a week, until the cage is well on its way. After that, you are free to go anywhere you wish."

Well, he took me up to this stone fortress of his, and gave me my own room and three squares a day, and every afternoon he stopped by to play chess with me until he caught me moving one of his pieces when I thought he wasn't looking, and after the week was up he gave me one final breakfast and had one of his men drive me into Peking.

I read a few weeks later that there was a real live dragon on display in Sydney, so I figured Doctor Aristotle Ho had gotten the funds he needed to conquer the world, but as you will see, I was just a little too preoccupied to worry much about it at the time.

4. THE GREAT WALL

The very first thing I learned in Peking is that Chinamen like games of chance every bit as much as white Christian gents do. The very last thing I learned in Peking is that they are even quicker to spot a marked deck of cards than your average American or European. The two learning experiences came about twenty minutes apart, and before the morning was half over I was back on the road, looking for some new place to settle down and build my Tabernacle.

It was about this time that China was pretty much divided up into kingdoms, and each kingdom was ruled by a warlord, which may have been a little harsh on some of the local citizenry but sure saved a lot of time and effort at the ballot box, and it occurred to me that after all the time they spent fighting each other, at least some of the armies were probably in need of some spiritual comforting, such as could only be brung to them by a sensitive and caring man of the cloth, such as myself.

I'd picked up a smattering of Chinese while on my way from Macau to Peking, so once I was a few miles out of the city I stopped an old man who was taking his cow out for a walk, and asked him where the nearest warlord had set up shop.

He told me that a General Sim Chow's barracks were about forty miles south along the road we were on, but suggested that the warlord most in need of spiritual uplifting and best able to pay for it due to his propensity to trade in certain of his homeland's perishable commodities was General Ling Sen, whose headquarters were many days' march to the west.

I thanked him for his time and trouble, and decided that I'd give General Sim Chow the first crack at my services, since he was so much closer. I began reappraising the situation when I came to a pile of bodies about ten miles later, and when I saw a Christian mission on fire a mile after that, I decided that General Ling Sen sounded so deeply in need of salvation that there wasn't no time to waste, so I took a hard right and started walking west.

I'd gone maybe seven or eight miles when I heard a drunken voice singing "God Save the King," except when I got close enough to make out the words it was more like "God Save the Liverpool Ruggers Team," which truth to tell made a lot more sense, as the Liverpool Ruggers Team was in fifth place in the standings the last time I'd seen a paper in Macau, whereas the King didn't have no serious competition for the throne that I was aware of.

I kept walking and came upon an English soldier, all dolled up in his parade best, with a bright red jacket and a pith helmet, sitting by the side of the road, drinking from a bottle of rice wine.

"Come join me, friend," he said when he looked up and saw me, and being the good-natured Christian that I am, I moseyed over and took a swig from his bottle.

"Are we still in China?" he asked after a moment.

"Unless they moved Peking when I wasn't looking, it's half a day's march from here," I answered.

"Damn!" he said. "I don't think the wine will hold out." He lowered his voice, and pointed to a backpack full of wine bottles. "I'm drinking my way back to jolly old England."

"Ain't you attached to some army unit or other?" I asked.

He shook his head unhappily. "They're all lost but me. I went out on a bit of a bender last month, and when I came back everyone was missing. So now I'm going back to England to report that my entire unit has gone A.W.O.L., and I alone am escaped to tell thee." He reached his hand out. "Merriweather's the name," he added. "Corporal Marmaduke Merriweather."

"The Right Reverend Doctor Lucifer Jones at your service," I replied, shaking his hand.

"Did you say *doctor*?" he said. "I've got a boil on my back that could use lancing."

"I ain't that kind of doctor," I answered. "I suppose I could recite some of Queen Sheba's racier amorous escapades over it, if you think that might help."

He considered it for a moment, then finally shook his head. "No, I think not. When all is said and done, it's the lot of the British soldier to suffer pain quietly and nobly."

"Well, you got the noble part down pat, Brother Merriweather, but I heard you singing from half a mile away."

"I keep hoping my army might hear me," he responded glumly.

Well, I took another drink just as a show of solidarity and sympathy, and then he took one, and before long we'd finished that bottle and another one, and then night fell and we slept beneath a tree alongside the road, and when morning came he decided to walk along with me until he came across his unit or England, whichever came first.

"Well, that's right neighborly of you," I said. "I always feel safer in the company of His Majesty's armed forces."

"And well you should," he replied. "Of course, I traded my rifle for the wine, and I seem to have misplaced my ammunition, but still, it's my function in life to protect all things British."

"I don't want to cause you no serious moral consternation, Brother Merriweather," I said, "but I ain't British."

"You speak British," he said. "That's enough for me." He paused for a moment. "By the way, Reverend Jones, I know where *I'm* going, but you haven't told me where you're heading yet."

"I'm seeking the headquarters of General Ling Sen," I said, "to offer them poor beleaguered soldiers a fighting shot at spiritual atonement."

"If you will accept a gentle word of advice," said Merriweather, "spiritual atonement probably does not rank very high up on General Ling Sen's list of priorities."

"Oh?" I said. "You know something about him?"

He shook his head. "I know absolutely nothing about him."

"Then how do you figure that he's not in the market for a preacher?"

"The mere fact that I haven't heard of him means that no one who has had any dealings with him has lived long enough to pass on that information to us." He shrugged. "Still, I suppose it's in our best interest to seek him out."

"It is?" I asked, since he had just loaded me down with a mighty tall heap of misgivings.

He nodded. "I'm already out of money, and I'll be out of rice wine in another few days. Possibly I can hire on as an advisor."

"What kind of combat do you specialize in, Brother Merriweather?" I asked.

"Combat?" he repeated. "Do you think I joined the army to *fight*? I'm an accountant."

"An accountant?"

"*Some*body has to pay for the uniforms and weapons and bullets and transportation and consumables," he replied. "I mean, Empire is all very well and good, Reverend Jones, but only if it can remain cost-effective."

"And you figure this here General Ling Sen is in serious need of an accountant?" I asked him.

"He's got an army to run, hasn't he?" answered Merriweather. "Why, with the things I could teach him about double-entry bookkeeping alone, he could continue to devastate the countryside for an extra three or four months at no additional cost."

Well, we kept on walking and drinking from Merriweather's diminishing supply of rice wine, and he kept trying to explain the more esoteric principles of tax-loss carry-forwards to me, and one day kind of melted into another, until one morning about a month later we came smack-dab up against this great big wall and couldn't go no farther.

"Looks like General Ling Sen don't take kindly to visitors," I opined as I looked both right and left and couldn't see the end of the wall nowhere in sight.

"With a wall like this around his barracks, one might say that he seems absolutely hostile to them," agreed Merriweather.

"Still," I said, "a man who can build a wall this big probably ain't exactly destitute."

"True," added Merriweather. "In fact, he's probably more in need of an accountant than most."

"And if this here wall is half as long as it looks to be, I got a feeling General Ling Sen ought to be happy to pay for a little heavenly insurance to make sure it don't get wiped out by earthquakes or floods or other such disasters as God is inclined to bring to them who don't toss a few coins into the poorbox every now and then."

"I do believe we're in business, Reverend Jones," said Merriweather.

Just then I heard some feet shuffling, which one hardly ever tends to hear when standing on grass like we was, so I looked up and, sure enough, there were three Chinese soldiers looking down on us from atop the wall.

"What are you doing here?" asked one of them in Chinese.

"Just looking for General Ling Sen's headquarters," I answered.

"Why?"

"We've come all the way from across the sea to bring him spiritual and fiduciary comfort," I said. "If you guys work for him, why don't you run off and tell him his lucky day has arrived?"

The three of them conferred for a long minute, and then one ran off along the top of the wall and the other two trained their rifles on us.

"Do not move," said one of them. "We must decide what to do with you."

A minute later a door opened about fifty feet away, and the soldier who had run off stepped out of the wall and motioned us to come to him. When we got there, we found ourselves facing half a dozen armed soldiers, who escorted us up this winding staircase, and after we climbed up maybe fifty feet or so, we stepped out through another door onto the top of the wall, which was a lot broader than it looked from the ground.

I heard a motor off to my left, and when I turned I saw a brand-new Bentley sedan driving right toward us. I was still wondering how they managed to get it onto the wall in the first place when it came to a stop and a big fat Chinaman stepped out, his chest and most of his belly all covered with medals.

"I have been told that you wish to speak with me," he said in English.

"We do if you're General Ling Sen," I said.

"General Ling Sen is no longer in charge here," he said. "I am General Chang."

"Well," I said with a shrug, "it ain't like General Ling Sen was a close personal friend or nothing. This here is Corporal Marmaduke Merriweather of His Majesty's armed forces, and I'm the Honorable Doctor Jones, internationally-known man of the cloth." Which was probably true, since there were still warrants out for my arrest in Illinois and Egypt and Morocco and Kenya and the Congo and South Africa, and I didn't suppose they could all have forgotten me so soon.

"Doctor *Lucifer* Jones?" he said.

"Now how'd you come to know that?" I asked, surprised.

He smiled. "Your reputation precedes you, Doctor Jones," he answered. "Already you have become something of a legend in Hong Kong and Macau."

"You don't say."

"I very much do say," replied General Chang. He turned to Merriweather. "And what have we here—a deserter from the British army?"

"*They* deserted me!" replied Merriweather. "*I'm* still here at my post."

"Why have you sought me out, Doctor Jones?" asked General Chang.

"I hear tell you run a territory of considerable size and complexity," I said, "so I just naturally figured that such a big bunch of ignorant yellow heathen—meaning no offense—would probably be in dire need of spiritual uplifting and maybe a nightly bingo tournament, the profits of which the Tabernacle of Saint Luke would be more than happy to split with the employer of these poor lost souls."

"And you?" asked General Chang, turning back to Merriweather.

"I should like to enlist in your army," said Merriweather.

"Good. We can always use more men. I trust that you're accomplished at garroting and gouging out eyes?"

"Well, actually, my specialty is accountancy," said Merriweather.

"*Our* specialty is conquest, pillage and rape," said General Chang. "You'll just have to adjust." He turned to two of his men. "Take him away and see that he's properly equipped."

"But—" began Merriweather.

"No, please don't thank me," said General Chang, as they began ushering Merriweather away. "All I ask is total, unquestioning loyalty and obedience. You can keep your gratitude for another occasion."

"So, General," I said, when Merriweather was out of earshot, "have we got a deal?"

"I think not, Doctor Jones," said General Chang. "Christianity is such a sterile, repressed religion."

"Not the way I practice it," I assured him.

"The answer is no," he said firmly. "Which is not to say that I might not have some other use for you."

"Long as the pay is good and it don't involve no heavy lifting, I suppose the Good Lord could spare me for a couple of weeks," I answered.

"Come with me back to my quarters," he said, signaling his car to turn around. "We'll talk as we drive."

"Suits me," I said, climbing into the Bentley. "By the way, just where is this kingdom of yours?"

"You're on it."

"I mean, how far does it extend?" I asked, looking off at the hills that rose up in the distance.

"Hundreds of miles," he replied.

"Really?" I said. "You must own half of China."

"Even better," he said with a smile. "I own a six-hundred-mile section of the Great Wall. Any traffic from one side to the other must pay me a healthy tribute."

"Yeah?"

He nodded. "And it just so happens that our most fertile poppy fields are on the west side of the wall, while our best markets for them are on the east side." He paused. "In truth, I cannot take credit for it. It was General Ling Sen who first saw the potential of taking control of the Wall, and of course the Wall itself was built to be easily defended." He lit up a cigar. "Yes, there's no question of it: General Ling Sen was a visionary of the highest order."

"What happened to him?" I asked.

"Ah, poor General Ling Sen!" said General Chang with feeling. "Surrounded by selfish, disloyal officers, he was betrayed by the most vicious of them."

"Who was that?" I asked.

"Me," said General Chang. "It was a dreadful, villainous, despicable thing to do, and if I had the slightest vestige of a conscience, I am quite certain I would be thoroughly ashamed of myself." He smiled at me. "However, to be perfectly candid with you, I must confess that I am enjoying the consequences of my unspeakable actions beyond my wildest expectations."

"Well, they say confession is good for the soul," I replied. "It strikes me that you're doing your poor blackened soul a heap of good just by telling me all this."

"You are a man after my own heart, Doctor Jones," said General Chang. "It is so rare that I meet anyone with whom I see eye to eye—and then, when I do, I am usually forced to kill him before he can do the same to me."

It seemed like a good time to change the subject, so I asked him exactly what kind of work he had in mind for me.

"As you know, Doctor Jones, my kingdom is some six hundred miles long."

"So you said."

"On the other hand, it is only sixty-five feet wide. That means that"—he pulled a pencil and paper out of a pocket and did some quick calculating—"the full extent of my kingdom is less than seven square miles."

"But as real estate goes, they're *prime* miles," I pointed out.

"Nevertheless, I have decided to expand my empire."

"Gonna take over more of the wall?" I asked.

He shook his head. "No matter how much of the wall we own, we remain at the mercy of anyone who wishes to lay siege to us. I have decided that it is time to take over General How Kung's territory."

"Where is this General How Kung located?" I asked.

He pointed out the window to the west. "He owns everything your eye can see, and beyond. If I had *his* territory, not only could I be assured of feeding my men, but I would never have to worry about fighting a two-front war." He smiled at me. "That's where *you* come in."

"Me?"

"Yes, Doctor Jones. For reasons I cannot fathom, General How Kung distrusts me; probably he is still carrying a childish grudge simply because I burned his village and stole his wife. At any rate, *you* shall be my emissary." He paused. "You will seek him out, guarantee his safety, agree to any conditions he sets, and get him to come and meet with me." Suddenly he smiled. "Then, after I murder him, I shall pay you the sum of one thousand British pounds."

"I don't want to throw no spanner in the works," I said cautiously, "but ain't this General How Kung likely to have some friends and relations that might consider such treatment unnecessarily harsh?"

"We live in a Darwinian world, Reverend Jones," replied General Chang. "To the victor belongs the spoils. How do you think How Kung *got* to be a general in the first place?" The Bentley came to a stop in front of a guardhouse that had been built into the wall. "Ah! Here we are. Would you care to join me in a drink?"

Plotting to kill Chinese warlords can be pretty thirsty work, so I got out of the car with him and followed him into his house, where he pulled out a bottle of whiskey while I was admiring all the treasures he had picked up during his travels. He poured us each a large glass, and we got to talking about this and that, and pretty soon he was asking me all about my adventures on the Dark Continent and I was asking him all about his wars of conquest, and suddenly it was getting on to midnight and we were on our third bottle.

"I'm feeling dizzy," said General Chang, getting kind of unsteadily to his feet. "I think I need a breath of fresh air."

"Sounds good to me," I said, getting up and following him out onto the wall.

"Lovely night," said General Chang, staggering just a bit. "It was on a night just like this that I killed General Ling Sen, poor fellow."

"How did you do it?" I asked.

He walked to the eastern edge of the wall. "I called him over to this very spot, told him I thought I saw someone prowling around on the ground, and then when he leaned over to look, I pushed him off."

I moseyed over to where he was standing and looked down. "That must be a good fifty feet or so," I said.

"It was a relatively painless death," said General Chang, starting to slur his words. "I don't believe he felt a thing for the first forty-nine feet."

"Maybe we ought to plant a cross or something to commemorate the unhappy event," I said.

"I like that," said General Chang. "Someday, hundreds of years from now, historians can come to the wall and see the very spot where I became a General. I like the way you think, Doctor Jones. Perhaps I shall permit you to become my biographer." He balanced himself precariously on the very edge of the wall and pointed down. "He hit the ground right there."

"By them little white flowers?" I asked.

"No," he said, peering into the darkness and swaying precariously. "It was right next to the bush."

"I can't see no bush," I said. "Maybe it's further down the wall."

"Nonsense," said General Chang. "I know where I pushed him off."

"Well, maybe the bush died, then," I said. "But all I can see is grass and some flowers."

"You must be even drunker than I am, Doctor Jones," he said irritably. "It's right down *there*."

He leaned over the wall and pointed, and suddenly he wasn't there any more, and a second later I heard a yell of "*Oh, shit!*" and then a loud thud, and I looked down and there was General Chang lying flat on his back fifty feet below me.

"We were *both* right," he mumbled just before he died. "The bush is in blossom."

Well, this turn of events caused me no little consternation, as you might imagine, especially since I wasn't the only one who had heard him fall. Suddenly soldiers began approaching me from every direction, and I suggested to my Silent Partner that if He had stockpiled any miracles in my heavenly account, this might be a pretty good time for me to cash a couple of them in.

The soldiers came to a stop a few feet away from me, and a couple of them walked over to the edge of the wall and looked down.

"You have killed General Chang!" said one of them in a shocked whisper.

"I can explain everything," I said. "It ain't my fault."

"Do not be so modest, General Jones," said another.

"*General* Jones?" I repeated.

"To the victor belongs the spoils," he said.

"Yeah?"

"You defeated General Chang in personal combat. That makes you our leader—at least, until someone defeats *you*."

I looked around and saw at least half a dozen oversized Chinamen who looked like they were chomping at the bit to do just that.

"What would have happened if he'd just gotten drunk and fell off the wall?" I asked.

"Since he was in your company, we'd probably put you to death for not protecting him."

"Well, as long as we're being open and aboveboard," I said, "I got to admit that he put up one hell of a fight. Not that the outcome was ever in doubt," I added for the benefit of those who were thinking of moving up in the ranks.

"He was our greatest warrior," said the soldier. "Many of our strongest men have challenged him, but none was ever victorious."

"All in a day's work," I said with becoming modesty.

The soldier turned to his companions. "General Chang is dead!" he yelled. "Long live General Jones!"

"Long live General Jones!" they all shouted back.

"Well, now, that's a right touching sentiment," I said. "And me and the Lord will certainly do our best to lead you to victory after victory." When the cheering had stopped, I explained to them that

I was going to set up housekeeping in General Chang's quarters while I plotted out our future conquests. That set off a whole new round of cheering, except for the five or six biggest of them, who had such lean and hungry looks whenever they stared at me that I decided it was time to leave the celebration and go to General Chang's guardhouse to consider my situation. A couple of minutes after I got there I heard a knock at the door, and then Marmaduke Merriweather let himself in.

"I heard the news," he said when he had closed the door behind him. "I suppose congratulations are in order."

"Thanks, Brother Merriweather," I said.

"If I may be so bold as to say so, I think a hasty retreat might be in even better order," he continued. "Somehow you don't seem to frighten them the way General Chang did."

"A couple of 'em are considering challenging me?" I asked.

"It's more like a couple of them *aren't*," he replied. "The rest are practically drawing straws to see who will be first."

"I was kind of afraid they might take that attitude," I said.

"It doesn't seem fair somehow," said Merriweather sympathetically. "I always thought that being a warlord was a lifetime position."

"Oh, it is, Brother Merriweather," I assured him. "The problem is that 'lifetime' seems to be a very elastic term in these here parts."

"What do you plan to do about it?" he asked.

"I'm still mulling on it," I said. "After all, I've only been the warlord for about twenty minutes. I ain't got all the nuances of the job nailed down yet."

"Well, as I see it," he said, "you've got two choices: you can flee to the east, or you can flee to the west."

"Running away is against my principles," I said. "Especially when there's a fortune in jade knick-knacks in the next room."

"But the only alternative is to fight every challenger," he pointed out.

"Well, I suppose that's what I'll have to do," I said, "me being the honorable Christian gentleman that I am."

"Meaning no disrespect," he said, "but if I were making book on the event, you'd be a fifty-to-one underdog against each and every opponent."

"That's what they said about old Jonah," I replied, "and he wound up harpooning the whale."

"I hate to correct you, Reverend Jones, but he wound up *inside* the whale," said Merriweather.

"Only in the British translation," I said. "Now, I appreciate your concern, Brother Merriweather, but my mind's made up. Get some of them soldiers in here so I can announce my intentions."

He shrugged and walked out onto the wall, then returned a minute later with a couple of soldiers in tow.

"You sent for us, General Jones?" asked one of them, snapping off a nifty salute.

"Yeah," I said. "It's come to my attention that some of the men think they can advance in rank pretty much the same way I did. Is that right?"

"I believe so, General Jones."

"I think we're gonna have to nip this in the bud," I said. "I want you to pass the word up and down the wall that I plan to take 'em all on, one at a time, comes morning."

"Our army extends for three hundred miles in each direction, General Jones," he replied. "It will take at least two days for word to pass up and down the ranks."

"All right," I said. "What's tomorrow?"

"Tuesday."

"Fine. You tell 'em that I'm going into training, and that on Thursday morning I plan to drive the Bentley to the south end of the army and work my way north, taking on all challengers one at a time."

"What about the ones who are outside right now?"

"They'll just have to wait their turn," I said. "After all, fair is fair. Tell 'em I should be able to get to them by Friday afternoon."

"You have that much confidence in your ability?" asked the soldier.

"I beat General Chang without working up a sweat, didn't I?" I answered.

Well, he didn't have no answer to that, so he just saluted and left and started spreading the word like I told him to.

"Is there anything I can do to help, Reverend Jones?" asked Merriweather when we were alone again.

"Well, I'd sure hate to be late for all these battles to the death," I said. "Why don't you spend the next couple of days making sure that the Bentley is all fueled up and in good working order?"

"I had in mind something more like lowering you down the side of the wall with a rope," he said.

"If Solomon had run from Goliath, where would we all be now?" I replied.

He just stared at me, sighed, shook his head, and walked out into the night. I locked the door behind him, spent the next couple of hours doing a quick inventory of General Chang's jade collection, and finally hunted up the bedroom and went to sleep.

I hung around the guardhouse for the next two days, finishing up General Chang's store of imported Scotch whiskey and watching Merriweather work on the Bentley. Just before sundown on Wednesday I wandered over to the building they were using for a mess hall, found an empty straw basket, and packed myself a big lunch so I wouldn't have to waste any time hunting up a restaurant between fights, and left a wake-up call for five in the morning.

I got up at about four o'clock, dumped the lunch under my bed, and filled up the basket with a pile of General Chang's better jade trinkets. Then I went out to where the Bentley was parked and put a couple of ten-gallon drums of gas into the trunk. Merriweather knocked on my front door at five on the dot, and I loaded the straw basket into the back seat, saluted the row of soldiers that were lined up to see me off, and climbed into the car beside him.

"Wake me when we've got about ten miles to go," I said as he headed off down the middle of the wall.

"How can you sleep at a time like this?" demanded Merriweather. "I'm a nervous wreck."

"Just relax and trust to the Lord," I said, closing my eyes and leaning back.

I must have fell sound asleep then, because the next thing I knew the car had come to a stop.

"Reverend Jones?" said Merriweather, shaking my shoulder gently.

"Yeah, what is it?"

"You said to let you know when we were within ten miles of our destination."

"Thanks," I said. "I'm gonna stretch and get some of the kinks out."

I opened the door and stepped out into the morning air. Some soldiers had gathered around, so I popped open the trunk and asked one of 'em to load the canisters of gasoline into the tank while I walked over to the edge of the wall and attended to a call of nature.

"I'll drive the rest of the way," I told Merriweather when I returned to the car. "It'll help get my reflexes sharp."

He scooted over to the passenger's side, and I spent the next couple of minutes getting used to the Bentley, which was a mighty fine car except that someone had gotten all mixed up and put the steering wheel and pedals on the wrong side.

"I wonder how fast this baby can go?" I said as we got to within two miles of my first fistic encounter.

"The speedometer goes up to one hundred and fifty," he answered.

"Is that miles or kilometers?" I asked.

He shrugged. "I don't know."

"Let's open her up and find out," I said, pressing the gas pedal down to the floor.

"Careful, Reverend Jones!" he yelled as we barreled along the top of the wall, sending soldiers jumping for cover. "You'll get us killed!"

"Only if I stop or slow down," I said sincerely, and suddenly we were past the last of the soldiers and Merriweather finally figured out what was happening and started laughing his head off. We heard some gunfire behind us, but whoever built that wall just didn't know when to call it quits, and we drove another four hundred miles before we finally ran out of gas and had to get out and start walking.

We came to a pair of towers in about half a mile, one on each side of the wall, each with a staircase leading down to the ground.

"Well, it's been a fascinating experience, Reverend Jones," said Merriweather, walking over to the staircase that led to the west, "but I've really got to continue my journey to England. The sooner they know the army is missing, the sooner they can send out search parties."

Somehow the notion of foot-slogging across the Gobi Desert didn't seem as appealing to me as it did to him, so I bid him farewell and clambered down the stairs on the east side of the wall, all set to sell General Chang's jade baubles to the highest bidder so I could finally get around to building my tabernacle.

5. THE ABOMINABLE SNOWMAN

I spent the next week walking south, since I had the Gobi to the west and a bunch of warlords to the east. I kept thinking that a town ought to pop into view any minute, but I didn't see anything except a bunch of farm fields and an occasional former warlord being hung out to dry, and I began thinking that my picnic basket could have used a little less jade and a little more lunch.

I was sitting down in the shade of a tree, thinking that whoever had called China a crowded country hadn't actually tried walking across it, when I heard a familiar voice coming from behind me.

"Well, I'll be damned if it ain't the Reverend Lucifer Jones!"

I got to my feet and turned around and found myself facing Capturing Clyde Calhoun, decked out in his usual khakis and pith helmet and leading a safari column.

"Well, howdy, Clyde," I said. "I ain't seen you since Mozambique. What are you doing in these here parts?"

"Same as usual," he said, walking up and shaking my hand. "Collecting animals for my circus—them what survives getting captured, anyway. The rest go to museums and gourmet chefs and other interested parties."

"I ain't seen hide nor hair of any animals since I got here," I said.

"Well, they take a heap of finding," he said. "But I just picked up seventy-three giant pandas from the bamboo forest up north."

"That's a lot of pandas," I said. "I hear tell they're an endangered species."

"They are *now*," he agreed, patting his rifle fondly.

"Maybe you should have left some for the Chinese," I suggested.

"Oh, I left 'em enough to breed," he assured me. Suddenly he frowned. "Unless both of 'em was females." He took a swig from his canteen, and then offered it to me. "How about yourself, Lucifer?" he continued as I took a long drink of water. "What are you doing out here in the middle of China?"

"Mostly looking for a way out," I admitted.

"Well, I'm headed for Tibet," he said. "Why don't you come along with me? I could use a little companionship; none of my bearers speak any American."

"What's so special about Tibet?" I asked.

"That's where we'll find the Abominable Snowman," he replied.

"Sounds ugly," I said. "Or at least sadly lacking in manners."

"He's worth a pretty penny back in the States," confided Calhoun. "Fifty grand stuffed and mounted, and at least twice that much if he's still mildly alive and twitching." He paused for a minute. "Tell you what: you come along with me, and I'll not only give you three squares a day, but I'll split the take with you if you find him first."

Which suddenly made Tibet start looking a whole lot more interesting.

"Clyde," I said, "you got yourself a deal. What's for lunch?"

He had a couple of his people set up a table and his chef whipped us up some panda sandwiches, and we washed 'em down with a few beers and got to reminiscing about old times, and before we knew it it was getting dark, so we wound up spending the night right there. We were up bright and early the next morning, and we made pretty good time, especially considering that Clyde had this habit of stopping every couple of minutes to shoot birds or squirrels or anything else that had this regrettable tendency to breathe in and out. I kept expecting to run into some warlord or other, but Clyde kept shooting so much that all the local warlords must have figured the Imperial Army was on the march and hightailed it out of our path, because we didn't see nary a one during the whole trek.

After a couple of months it started getting right chilly at night, and pretty soon the days weren't much warmer, and finally we had to stop long enough to make us a pair of fur coats out of panda skins. When we finally hit the Kunlun Mountains, Clyde paid off about eighty of his bearers and skinners and sent 'em packing, and just kept a cook and a couple of trackers with us.

Now, it's entirely possible that there's a piece of level ground somewhere in Tibet, but if there is, I never did see it. We started following footpaths up the mountains, hunting for a pass to the other side, where Clyde was sure he could get a line on the Abominable Snowman in a little town called Saka, but once we found the pass all it did was lead us out of the Kunlun Mountains into the Tangkula Mountains, which were even higher and colder, and before long we were sitting in a cave at about ten thousand feet in the middle of a howling blizzard, warming our hands next to a fire he'd built and trying real hard not to listen to our teeth chattering.

The weather had cleared by morning, and as we wandered out of the cave we came upon some tracks in the snow.

"Looks like we had some polar bears hanging around last night," I said.

"Ain't no polar bears in Tibet," answered Clyde, squatting down and examining them. "These here tracks was made by something what walks upright, and stands maybe eight feet tall." He looked up at me with a great big smile. "I don't think we're gonna have to go to Saka after all. I think maybe we just lucked out and are sharing this mountain with the Abominable Snowman."

"Yeah?"

He nodded vigorously. "Let's split up forces and go out searching for him. I'll follow his tracks, and you go the other direction just in case he circled around, and we'll meet back at the cave at nightfall."

He started walking off.

"Ain't you gonna take your gunbearer or your tracker with you?" I asked.

"Too dangerous," he shouted back. "Best to leave this kind of work to experienced hunters."

"I don't want to cast no pall of gloom on the proceedings, Clyde, but I ain't an experienced hunter, or even an inexperienced one if push comes to shove."

"Then wait in the cave with the others. I'll be back in a few hours."

Which made excellent sense, and which is what I did.

Clyde piled in at twilight, with little icicles hanging down from his moustache, and immediately sat down by the fire.

"How'd it go?" I asked, since I didn't see no snowman, abominable or otherwise, in tow.

"The tracks vanished about a mile from here," he said, holding his hands out to warm them. "I spent most of the afternoon hunting for his lair, but I couldn't find it." He paused thoughtfully. "I think tomorrow I'll lay some traps for him."

"Tell me more about this here Snowman," I said.

"Ain't that much to tell," answered Clyde. "The locals call him the Yeti, and near as I can figure out he spends most of his time hanging around the mountain doing abominable things."

"Anybody ever seen him?"

"Probably," said Clyde, "but I get the distinct impression that them what's actually encountered him have passed on to the next plane of existence with remarkable alacrity."

"I wonder what he eats?" I mused, hoping that he hadn't developed a taste for Christian missionary somewhere along the way.

"Beats me," said Clyde. "If it's anything but snow and rocks, he must be one hungry snowman." Suddenly he looked up. "Say, you gave me an idea, Lucifer. I think I'll bait some of them traps with the last of the panda meat."

I told him I thought it was a good plan, especially since I'd had my fill and then some of panda steaks, and then we turned in, and the next morning Clyde was out laying his traps as soon as the sun came up.

I asked Kim, our cook, to fix me up some coffee. He came back a couple of minutes later with a pot of tea.

"I said I wanted coffee," I told him.

"Coffee all gone," he said. "You drink tea."

I didn't think no more of it, but when Clyde went out the next morning to bait more traps, I asked for tea, and this time what I got was a pitcher of hot water.

"Tea all gone too," explained Kim.

"Just how much tea did Clyde drink last night?" I asked.

"Him no drink tea at night. Just whiskey."

"Maybe he took it with him this morning," I suggested.

"Twenty pounds of it?" replied Kim.

That did seem like a lot of tea, no matter how eleven o'clockish Clyde might feel, so I got to thinking, and it didn't take me long to figure out that someone was swiping our supplies. And since the bearer and the tracker hadn't gone out in two days and there wasn't no place inside the cave to stash it, I figured it had to be someone else.

And since there was only one other person who was crazy enough to be wandering around on the mountain in this weather, I decided that things were suddenly looking up for my bank account.

Clyde returned at sunset, and immediately started warming himself by the fire.

"How'd it go?" I asked.

"Oh, he's out there all right," answered Clyde. "And he's a smart one, too."

"How so?"

"He managed to pick up one of the panda steaks without getting snared. I'll have to camouflage my traps better."

We talked for a while, settled down for a hard evening's drinking, and fell asleep just about the time the nightly blizzard started blowing.

The next morning I waited until Clyde had left, then told Kim to fix me up a dozen sandwiches. While he was busy making them, I got into my panda coat and picked up one of Clyde's auxiliary rifles. When Kim was done, I put the sandwiches into a backpack, and then, as an afterthought, I added twelve bottles of beer, and told him I was going out for a little exercise and to maybe hunt up a grocery store.

I saw Clyde's footprints heading off to the left, so I turned right and began following a narrow ridge that wound its way down the mountain. I stopped about every half mile, took a sandwich and a beer out of my backpack, and placed them on the snow. After about three miles the path I was on started branching every which way, but that didn't bother me none since all I had to do to get back was turn around and follow my footprints, so I just kept on wandering and setting down sandwiches and beer.

The snow was right deep, and the altitude wasn't exactly a boon to serious breathing, and by the time I'd emptied my backpack I figured it was getting on toward midafternoon, so I turned around and started heading back to the cave.

I'd gone about half a mile, and was just turning a corner around a big boulder, when I saw this huge shaggy figure, maybe eight feet high, standing about two hundred yards away with its back to me, eating a sandwich and washing it down with a beer. I figured the safest course was to fire a warning shot, just to kind of get its attention and let it know I was armed, so I pointed the rifle straight up at the sky and pulled the trigger.

I think I ought to break into my narrative at this point to make a suggestion born of bitter experience: if you ever find yourself on a narrow ledge of a snow-covered mountain in Tibet, firing a .550

Nitro Express into the air probably ain't the smartest course of action available to you.

When I woke up, I felt kind of constricted. I thought I heard the sounds of digging, but I couldn't move, or even turn my head, to see what was happening. Then, after a couple of minutes had passed, I felt two huge hands grab me by the shoulders and pull me up through the snow, and suddenly I was facing this great big guy who was wearing a shaggy coat made out of sheepskin.

"All right," he said, holding me off the ground by my shoulders and shaking me. "Who are you?"

"The Right Reverend Doctor Lucifer Jones."

"You're from Guido Scarducci, right?" he said, finally putting me down.

"I ain't never heard of him," I said, brushing myself off.

"Then why did you shoot at me?" he demanded.

"I thunk you was the Yeti."

"What's a Yeti?" he asked.

"Well, as near as I can tell, a Yeti is you," I said. "Except it sure sounds to me like you're speaking one hundred percent pure American."

"Of course I am," he said. "I was raised in Butte, Montana."

"What's a fellow American doing on a mountain in Tibet?" I asked.

"It's a long and tragic story, Doctor Jones," he said, sitting down on a big rock. "My name is Sam Hightower. By the time I was fifteen years old I was seven feet tall and still growing, so I figured that playing basketball was my calling in life, and as soon as I got out of high school I latched onto a semi-pro team called the Butte Buccaneers. About a week before we were scheduled to play the Great Falls Geldings for the championship, for which we were a real big favorite, a gambler called Guido Scarducci came up and offered me five thousand dollars to make sure we didn't win by more than ten points."

"No sense embarrassing the other team," I said sympathetically.

"Those were my feelings precisely," said Hightower. "The problem is that the next night, another gambler named Vinnie Bastino offered me twenty thousand to make sure we won by fifteen points or more."

"I can see where that might present a serious moral and economic dilemma," I said.

"Well, I was young and innocent and didn't view it as such," said Hightower. "I just figured I'd pay Mr. Scarducci his five thousand back out of my earnings and we'd be all square and there'd be no hard feelings and we might even have a laugh about it over a drink or two."

"I take it he didn't quite see it that way?" I said.

"I realized he and I had a little communications problem when he blew up my car and set fire to my apartment that night," said Hightower. "And when he missed me and shot six of my teammates during the victory parade the next day, I figured it was probably time to take my leave of the fair city of my birth, so I hopped the first train heading east, and wound up in New York." He paused. "Problem is, he found me there, too. And in London. And in Rome. I finally decided that it's not all that easy to disappear in a crowd when you're eight foot two inches tall, so after he found me again in Athens, I made up my mind to go where there weren't any crowds at all, and I've been living on this damned mountain for six years now, waiting for Guido Scarducci to hunt me down."

"You hang around here much longer and you're gonna get yourself hunted by a lot more people than Guido Scarducci," I told him.

"Why?" he asked. "Surely borrowing a little coffee and tea isn't a capital offense even in Tibet."

"This ain't got nothing to do with coffee or tea," I said. "You ever hear of the Abominable Snowman?"

"I heard legends when I was growing up, just like I heard about Bigfoot and Paul Bunyan."

"Well, most folks in these parts think you're him."

"Why on earth should they think that?" he asked, kind of bewildered.

"Well, the notion of an eight-foot basketball player hiding out from gamblers on top of a mountain in Tibet probably ain't had time to take root yet," I explained.

"Yeah," he said thoughtfully. "Now that I come to consider it, I can see your point. I assume that's why you were shooting at me?"

I nodded. "After all, you did go for my bait."

"You know how hard it is to find food up here?" he replied. He rubbed his jaw. "And I damned near broke a tooth on that frozen meat you put out yesterday."

"I didn't put it out," I said. "Which reminds me—we'd better get back to my cave so I can tell Capturing Clyde not to shoot you."

"Capturing Clyde *Calhoun?*" he said excitedly.

"You've heard of him?"

"I've seen all his movies and read all his books," said Hightower. "He's one of my boyhood heroes."

"I'm sure he'll be mighty glad to hear it," I said.

"But surely I'm not in any danger from him," continued Hightower. "I mean, doesn't Capturing Clyde always bring 'em back alive?"

"Well, now, that's subject to various delicate shades of interpretation," I said. "But I think it's fair to say that them what he brings back without eating or skinning first is generally alive. Still," I added, "if I was you, I'd introduce myself to him right quick, and preferably when he wasn't carrying his gun."

He stood up and looked up the mountain.

"I'm afraid that won't be possible, Doctor Jones," he said.

"Why not?" I asked.

"Because when you fired your rifle you started an avalanche that seems to have brought down half the mountain. We could be days or even weeks getting back to your cave."

"What are we going to do in the meantime?" I asked.

"I've got shelters hidden all over the mountain," answered Hightower. "We'll find one that hasn't been covered by the avalanche and use it for a headquarters while we try to clear the trail to your cave."

Well, I couldn't think of no better alternative, and so I followed him to one of his shelters, where he had a fire going and an old hand-cranked Victrola and lots of Rudy Vallee records, which weren't really to my taste but were a lot better than just sitting there listening to the wind whistle by.

He was real interested in finding out what events of Earth-shaking import had transpired since he'd left the States in rather a hurry, so I told him about how the Red Sox had traded Babe Ruth to the Yankees, and how Clara Bow had encouraged the Southern California football team to win the Rose Bowl, and that one of our Presidents had died but I couldn't remember which one. He was especially glad to hear that Morvich had won the 1922 Kentucky Derby.

"I put all my money on him just before I took off," he explained.

"Well, you ought to have a tidy nest egg waiting for you when you finally go home," I said.

"I doubt it," he replied with a sigh. "My bookie was Guido Scarducci."

"Maybe there's some subtle little nuance I'm missing here," I said, "but ain't Guido Scarducci the fellow that's out to kill you?"

"Yes."

"Then why on earth did you bet your money at his particular establishment?"

Hightower shrugged. "He was the only bookie in Montana."

I suddenly found myself silently agreeing that Tibet was probably just the place for him to hang out while his survival skills were catching up with the rest of his growth, but I kept these sentiments to myself since I make it a practice never to offend anyone over eight feet tall unless it ain't avoidable.

The nightly blizzard came and went, and we were out at sunrise the next morning, digging a path up to Clyde's cave. It wasn't all that hard to dig through the snow, but every half hour or so we'd come to a boulder that we couldn't climb over or walk around, and as you might imagine it kind of slowed our progress. Hightower was afraid Clyde might be trapped in his cave, but I figured that Clyde was used to taking care of himself in strange lands and ticklish situations, and in truth the one thing that kept me going through all them days of digging and shoving boulders down the mountainside was the thought of all that jade sitting there in my picnic basket.

After a week we ran out of food and had to change shelters, and after two more weeks *all* the shelters were plumb out of food, and we figured if we didn't reach Clyde in another day or two we were going to have to climb down the mountain and borrow a little food from some of the locals. Hightower assured me that it wouldn't be no problem, since whenever they saw him they started screaming and running the other way, which up to now had made him think he should maybe have packed some deodorant when he left Athens, but which he finally realized was just their reaction to him being the Abominable Snowman.

Anyway, we finally cleared the way to Clyde's cave on the twenty-second day, and much to our surprise we found that it was deserted, except for a note and some kind of printed ticket that he'd stuck onto the wall right near the entrance, and which I picked up and read as follows:

Dear Lucifer:

I went out looking for you after I heard the shot, but I soon saw that you were probably buried under half the mountain. If that is true and you are dead, then read no further, but if you are alive and manage to make your way back here, I should tell you that after waiting a week for you to show up I have figgered that you and the Yeti are both dead, and have therefore decided to make tracks for Australia, where I got me a commission to hunt down a few hundred koala bears. At least they figure to make better eating than panda meat. (Ho ho.)

It seems a shame to leave all your jade doodads to rot here in the cave, so I am taking them with me back to civilization and will buy a drink to your sainted memory with some of the profits when I sell them. And just in case you ain't dead, I want you to know that I am a honorable man what would never rob a friend, and I am leaving you a lifetime pass to Capturing Clyde's Circus and Wild Animal Show in exchange for taking the trinkets with me.

Your Pal (or Rest in Peace, whichever is applicable),

Clyde Calhoun

I crumpled up both the letter and the lifetime pass and threw them to the floor of the cave.

"The son of a bitch ran off with my jade!" I said.

"You can't eat jade," said Hightower unhappily. "He might at least have left us some food."

"Well, we got no money and we got no food," I said. "I reckon it's time we took our leave of this here mountain."

"Where will we go?" asked Hightower. "I'm still a wanted man, you know."

"Well, there's no sense going back north into China," I said. "They'd probably just ask a bunch of bothersome questions about General Chang's knick-knacks. I figure our best bet is to head south."

"If we go south we'll run into the Himalayas," said Hightower.

"Religious sects don't bother me none," I replied confidently. "I'll convert 'em in no time flat."

I walked out of the cave and started heading south, having wasted the better part of three months and a modest fortune in jade while wandering around the countryside with Clyde, and I promised my Silent Partner that the next time I took charge of a wall or an army or anything big like that, I was setting up shop and finally building my Tabernacle.

But as you will soon see, it wasn't quite as easy as it sounds.

6. THE LAND OF ETERNAL YOUTH

It took Hightower and me another month before we hit anything resembling civilization, at which time we found ourselves in Katmandu, which has a real exotic name but truth to tell ain't a lot different from Boise or Dubuque, except that it's a hell of a lot colder in the summers, and hardly any of the locals speak English.

Still, mathematics is a universal language, and I soon replenished our coffers in a series of friendly little contests involving pasteboards and various combinations of the number Twenty-one. It was only after a couple of disgruntled losers started complaining that *my* deck added up to a lot more Twenty-ones than *their* decks did that I decided it was time to hit the road again.

"Where are you heading?" asked Hightower.

"Someplace warm," I said. "What's south of here?"

"India."

"Then that's where I'm heading."

"I can't go with you," he said.

"Why not?" I asked.

"From everything I hear, India's a pretty crowded place," he answered. "And the bigger the crowd, the more I stand out. I'll be much safer finding a nice little village in Nepal and settling down here."

"Guido Scarducci's probably forgot all about you by now," I said.

"Have you ever known a bookie to forget a debt?" he asked.

Well, I didn't have no quick and ready comforting answer to that, so I bid him good-bye, packed enough food for a month, and lit out of Katmandu just in time to avoid a tedious discussion about the laws of statistical averages with some of the locals. I made pretty good progress for a week or so, but then a major league blizzard came up, and by the time it ended two days later all the roads and trails were covered, and within another week I was forced to admit that I was about as lost as people ever get to be.

Then one day I came to a pass that led to a winding trail down a mountainside, and suddenly it wasn't so cold anymore, and before long the snow vanished and I was walking on grass. I could see a great big green valley stuck smack in the middle of the mountains, and I decided to head on over to it to see if I could rustle up a hot meal and maybe a friendly game of chance or two.

Just before I reached the valley I came to a rickety wooden bridge leading over a stream, and on the other side of it were a bunch of guys who looked kind of Chinese lining a path that led up to this enormous white temple, which in turn was surrounded by a batch of little white houses.

Well, they just stared at me without saying nothing, so I put on my friendliest smile and crossed the bridge and was about to introduce myself when the strangest damned thing happened: the second I got to their side of the creek, they all got to their knees and bowed their heads, which could have meant anything from them all being ready for a friendly game of craps to this being the quickest mass conversion in my experience as a man of the cloth.

Then a tall thin man came out of one of the houses and walked up to me.

"Greetings," he said. "I am Tard."

"Me, too," I said. "This place take a heap of getting to."

"You misunderstand me," he said. "Tard is my name."

"And I'm the Right Reverend Doctor Lucifer Jones at your service," I said. "Group weddings and funerals done cheap."

"We have been waiting for you, Doctor Jones," said Tard.

"You have?" I said.

"Yes," he replied. "Welcome to the kingdom of Shali-Mar."

"I don't recall seeing anyplace called Shali-Mar on any of the maps of the area," I said.

He just kind of chuckled at that. "You must be tired and hungry after your journey. I will have your rooms prepared while you are eating."

"Well, that's right neighborly of you, Brother Tard," I said.

"It is my job to serve you," he answered. "If there is anything you want, anything at all, you have but to tell me, and it shall be arranged."

"You act like this to all your guests?" I asked.

"You are our first visitor in almost two hundred years," he replied.

"Probably just as well," I said, admiring the sight of some young ladies walking through the fields with water pitchers on their heads. "If the travel agents ever find out about this place, they'll ruin it. Still," I added, "I don't know how you could have been expecting me. This little stopover wasn't exactly on my itinerary."

"Nonetheless, we have been expecting you, Doctor Jones." He paused. "Doesn't it strike you as unusual that everyone has knelt down the instant they have seen you?"

"Truth to tell, I been mulling on it, Brother Tard," I admitted. "I finally figured that they'd just never seen such a good-looking white man before, and didn't know quite what else to do about it."

He shook his head. "This is their traditional way of greeting the High Lama."

"He looks a lot like me, does he?" I asked.

"He has been dead for one hundred and thirty-four years," answered Tard. "But according to our legends, the day would come when a pale man from a distant land would cross over the bridge to Shali-Mar, and he would become the High Lama." He turned to me. "And now the legend has come true."

"Well, now, that's right interesting, Brother Tard," I said. "What does the job pay?"

"I don't think you understand, Doctor Jones," said Tard. "The High Lama is the absolute ruler of Shali-Mar. He is our physical master, and our conduit to God."

"The absolute ruler, you say?"

"That is correct."

I looked at a couple of nubile young maidens who were coming out of the temple and winked at one of 'em, who blushed and got down on her knees right quick. "The High Lama is your conduit to God?"

"That's right."

"And anything the High Lama says, goes?"

"Of course."

"Well, Brother Tard," I said, shooting him a great big smile, "your prayers have been answered. Talking to God is one of the best things I do, me being a man of the cloth and all." I pulled a cigar out of my pocket and lit it up while surveying my kingdom. "Why don't you join me for lunch and explain some of the intricacies of the job?"

"I am merely your chief administrator," said Tard. "It would be better for the High Priestess to discuss the more esoteric details of your position with you."

"Sounds good to me," I said. "I've always had a soft spot in my heart for High Priestesses."

We entered the temple, and I found myself face-to-face with a big golden statue of a lion which had rubies the size of golf balls for eyes and a bunch of diamonds for teeth. As I looked around, I saw a bunch of other little gem-covered trinkets that put General Chang's collection of jade knick-knacks to shame.

"Doctor Jones?" said Tard, after I'd spent a proper amount of time appreciating them. "Please follow me."

He led me through a batch of rooms, each bigger and finer than the last, and finally we came to one that had a huge table in the middle of it. At the center of the table was an ornate silver bowl filled with fruit.

"Please make yourself comfortable," said Tard. "I will go fetch the High Priestess." He walked to a doorway and turned to me. "She will be so happy to know that you have finally arrived, Doctor Jones. She has been waiting seventy years to instruct you."

"She's seventy years old?" I asked.

"No, she's much closer to one hundred and ten," answered Tard. "But she's only been the High Priestess for seventy."

Well, as you can imagine, this kind of dampened my enthusiasm, but I didn't see no way out of meeting with her, so I just pulled an apple out of the bowl and started munching on it, and about the time I was done I looked up and there in the doorway was this voluptuous young lady with long black hair and big brown eyes, all done up in a white silk outfit that didn't hide anywhere near as much as she seemed to think it did.

"Good afternoon, Doctor Jones," she said in the sweetest voice I ever did hear.

"It's getting better by the minute," I agreed. "What's your name?"

"Lisara," she said, giving me a great big toothy smile.

"Well, Lisara, honey," I said, "I got to meet with some wrinkled old High Priestess in the next couple of minutes, but once I get rid of her, what do you say to coming up to my room for an intimate little dinner for two?"

"I *am* the High Priestess, Doctor Jones," she said.

"I guess the thought of meeting with the High Lama was too much for the last one, huh?" I said. "Send my regrets to her family, and remind me to bring a wreath to the funeral."

"I have been the High Priestess for seventy years," she said.

"Come on," I said. "You can't be much more than nineteen or twenty years old."

"I am one hundred and eleven."

"You're kidding, right?"

"No, I truly am one hundred and eleven years old."

"Then how come you look like you do?" I asked.

"I avoid all fats and starches," she said, "and I jog five miles every morning."

"And that's all there is to it?"

"Well, that's why I look *fit*," she explained. "As for why I look *young*, it is because I live in Shali-Mar. This is the Land of Eternal Youth: no one ever ages here."

"Come to think of it, I didn't see no old codgers on the path up to the temple," I said.

"There aren't any," said Lisara. "The oldest of us all is Tard; he was alive when the last High Lama died." She paused. "It is something in the air, I think."

"Then why do you keep this place such a secret?" I asked. "You could put Miami Beach and the Riviera out of business."

"We have everything we need," she replied. "We have no desire to be overrun by outsiders."

"You could at least send a team to the Senior Olympics and clean up making side bets on 'em."

She shook her head sadly. "Once a citizen of Shali-Mar leaves, the aging process accelerates. Before he passes beyond the mountains that surround us, he is a gnarled and withered travesty of a human being."

"Yeah, I can see where that might present a problem or two," I said. "Especially in the sprints and high hurdles."

"But we have no wish to leave," she continued. "Our life here has been idyllic, and now that we once again have a High Lama, it will be perfect."

"Well, now that you brought the subject up," I said, "just what does the High Lama do?"

"You are our spiritual leader," she explained. "It is your job to probe the eternal verities."

"I can think of a lot of 'em that need probing," I agreed, getting into the spirit of it. "Like why do elevators all arrive at the same time? Or why does it always rain right after you wax your car? Why does traffic always move faster in the other lane?"

"Those are not precisely the ones I had in mind," she said.

"Why don't you come up to my room tonight?" I said, "We can discuss what you got in mind, plus a couple of things I got in mind."

"Oh, I couldn't do that, Doctor Jones," she said.

"Well, if it's a problem, I could come to your room," I said agreeably.

She shook her head. "The High Lama must avoid even the appearance of impropriety."

"What's the point of being the High Lama in the first place if I can't pay a social call on a lovely young lady when I'm of a mind to?" I asked.

"It simply isn't done," she said. "You are our spiritual leader."

"No reason why I can't do both," I said. "I always set aside Sunday mornings for saving souls."

"You do not understand, Doctor Jones," she said. "The High Priestess must forsake all earthly pleasures."

"That's kind of a rigid job qualification, ain't it?" I said.

"No one ever said that being the High Priestess was easy," she answered.

I made up my mind then and there to issue an executive order, or whatever it was High Lamas did, to the effect that it was okay for the High Priestess to indulge in a little hanky-panky from time to time, and was about to mention it to her when a couple of Lesser Priestesses arrived with lunch, and since I hadn't seen no cooked food for almost a month I sat right down and started eating away.

Tard came in just when I was finishing up dessert, and told Lisara that he had to prepare me for the inauguration or coronation or whatever gets done to them what is elected High Lama, and that she could continue talking to me at dinnertime. She bowed and left the room, and Tard sat himself down next to me.

"You will officially become our High Lama in a ceremony this afternoon," he said. "I think it would be best if you shaved and bathed before it begins. I'll have a couple of servants prepare your bath."

Well, you can imagine my disappointment when I found out that the servants were of the masculine persuasion, so I scrubbed right quick, shaved off three weeks' growth, and got into this white robe they'd laid out for me. I'd barely had time to light up a cigar when Tard came by and ushered me down to a huge open courtyard in the middle of the temple. It seemed like the whole town was there to greet me, all of 'em young and beautiful except for them what was young and handsome, and pretty soon Lisara showed up, looking better than ever, and started talking at me in some unfamiliar language, and then she and everyone else seemed to be waiting for an answer, so finally I said "I sure do!" and she put this gold amulet around my neck and then everyone knelt down again and suddenly I was the High Lama. I figured at least we'd have a few drinks to celebrate, and maybe do a little serious dancing, and I was already preparing a speech about how I was gonna clean up all the mistakes of the previous administration and lower taxes and put a chicken in every pot, when they all kind of wandered off back to their houses, and I was left alone with Tard and Lisara.

"That's it?" I said.

"It is accomplished," said Tard.

"Ain't there even no Inauguration Ball?" I asked.

"It would be anticlimactic after your investiture," said Tard.

"Are you trying to tell me that there little ceremony was the high point of the day?"

"For most of our people, it was the high point of their lives," said Lisara.

"Well, I can see we're gonna have to make some changes around here," I said.

"That might not be a wise idea," said Tard.

"I'm the High Lama, ain't I?" I said.

"Yes."

"As I understand it, that means that any idea I got is a quality idea."

"But you are supposed to spend your life in serene contemplation," said Tard.

"I been contemplating non-stop since I got here," I said. "I spent half the afternoon contemplating what that gold lion would be worth on the open market, and I spent the rest of it contemplating how much rent I could save the government by having Lisara move in with me."

"I don't think you understand your position, Doctor Jones," he said. "You are the High Lama of Shali-Mar."

"Right," I said. "And that means what I say goes."

"Within limitations," said Tard.

"Nobody ever mentioned no limitations for me when I applied for the job."

"Aren't you aware of the fact that you just took vows of poverty and celibacy in front of the entire community?" said Tard.

"I did *what?*"

"It's true, Doctor Jones," said Lisara. "That's what you agreed to at the end of the ceremony."

"I thought I was agreeing to be the High Lama!" I said.

"You were," she said. "And the High Lama is penniless and celibate."

I took off the amulet and handed it to Tard. "That being the case, I hereby resign from the High Lama business."

"You can't," he said.

"I just did."

"I urge you to consider the consequences of your actions," said Tard. "If you are not the High Lama, then you are just an intruder from the Outside World, and it is our obligation to kill you."

"Why?" I demanded. "What have I ever done to you?"

"We must keep our location secret, or we will be overrun with adventurers who will steal our women and loot our treasures."

"Let's calm down and be reasonable, Brother Tard," I said. "I can see why you don't want no foreign devils messing with your women or your trinkets, but it seems to me that a naturalized devil who also happens to be the High Lama ought to have a little more leeway."

"That's out of the question," he said, and then held out the amulet in one hand and drew his sword with the other. "You can be the High Lama, or you can be put to death. The choice is yours."

"Well," I said, staring at his sword, "I can see now that I may have been a little hasty in my previous decision. I suppose there's worse things than being the High Lama." First and foremost of which was the thought of getting cut up into fishbait.

Tard reached over and placed the amulet around my neck again. "You are young and hot-blooded and impetuous, as I once was," he said, putting his sword back in its sheath. "Fortunately, it's a phase that only lasts for two or three centuries."

"Well, that's a definite comfort, Brother Tard," I said glumly. "I think I'll take a walk around the kingdom and mull over everything you've said."

"Certainly, Doctor Jones," answered Tard. "Dinner will be served at sunset."

"Lisara, why don't you come with me to make sure I don't get lost?" I said.

"I am yours to command," she said. I must have looked right approving of that, because she quickly added, "Within limitations."

We started walking through the fields, and everywhere I went people kept kneeling down the second they saw me, and I tried to imagine a couple of centuries of seeing nothing but the tops of peoples' heads.

"Try not to be disappointed, Doctor Jones," said Lisara. "You will soon adjust to the contemplative life."

Well, truth to tell, for the past five minutes the only contemplating I'd been doing was how to get out of Shali-Mar with maybe a few diamonds and rubies for my trouble, and perhaps a handful of Lesser Priestesses for warmth and companionship of a cold winter's night, but Lisara was going on so rhapsodically about the pleasures of the mind that I figured that this probably wasn't the most propitious time to share my thoughts with her.

We got back to the temple just in time for dinner, and afterward Lisara went off to wherever it was that the Priestesses hung out, and Tard came up and asked me if there was anything he could do for me before I turned in.

"Well, now that you come to mention it, Brother Tard," I said, "I still got some questions about this whole set-up."

"Yes?"

I nodded. "Like, for example, nobody ever grows old or gets sick here, right?"

"That is correct."

"Then what did the last High Lama die of?"

"He tried to cross the bridge and leave Shali-Mar, and so I was forced to kill him," answered Tard.

"Was he a visitor, like me?" I asked.

He nodded. "So were the three before him."

"Let me guess: you killed them all for trying to leave?"

"Curious, isn't it?" said Tard. "That so many High Lamas would want to leave our little paradise?"

"Beats the hell out of me," I said.

"Was that all you wished to know, Doctor Jones?"

"I got a few more questions, if you got the time to answer them."

"Certainly," he said.

"Just out of curiosity," I said, "is there anything a High Lama can do that constitutes a firing offense, as opposed to a killing offense?"

"Absolutely nothing," he said. "As long as you obey your vows, you are virtually all-powerful in Shali-Mar."

Which was like telling me that as long as Exterminator didn't break no legs, he was a fair-to-middling racehorse.

"Is there anything else you wish to know, Doctor Jones?" he asked.

"No, I guess that's about it."

"If you need anything, just send for me," he said, bowing. "I am your servant."

Which was just when the Lord suggested to me that there was more than one way to skin a cat.

"Just a minute," I said.

"Yes, Doctor Jones?"

"Who appointed you my servant?"

"We are *all* your servants."

"Okay, then—who made you the chief administrator?"

"I have been chief administrator for more than three hundred years."

"But if I was to make an official pronouncement that you'd be better fit to clean the royal stables, you'd show up for work there tomorrow morning with a broom and a shovel, right?"

"Have I displeased you in some way, Doctor Jones?"

"Not a bit, Brother Tard," I said. "But I just did my first serious visualizing of the Cosmic All tonight, and for some reason I keep seeing you sweeping up behind horses."

"Why am I being demoted?" he asked.

"Don't view it as a demotion at all," I said. "If I was you, I'd consider it an opportunity to get back in touch with the common people—them what don't hold their noses and run the other way when you approach."

"Is this change in my status temporary or permanent?" he asked, kind of frowning.

"Well, seeing that no one ever gets old here, I think you can view it as temporary," I said. "I figure six or seven hundred years ought to do the trick."

He swallowed hard.

"One more thing," I said. "As your last official duty, pass the word that I'll be interviewing potential chief administrators tomorrow morning."

He stared at me and didn't say nothing, and since I'd said everything I had to say, I gave him a friendly pat on the shoulder and went up to my room.

Tard showed up maybe half an hour later. "Perhaps I was mistaken," he said.

"Yeah?"

"The High Lama is incapable of making an unwise decision," he said. "And since it is patently unwise to send such a qualified person as myself to work in the stables for the next five hundred years, you perforce cannot be the High Lama."

"I do believe you've hit the nail on the head, Brother Tard," I said.

"Therefore," he continued, "the best thing to do is sneak you out of here under cover of night."

"I was wondering how long it would take you to come around to that conclusion," I said.

"How soon can you be ready to leave?" he asked.

"I've been all packed for the past twenty minutes," I told him.

"Where is your luggage?"

"Right there on the bed," I said, pointing to my backpack.

"Excuse me for a moment," he said, and started rummaging through it. It was after he'd pulled out the fifteenth and last of the statues that he turned to me and said, "Did you plan to leave us *anything*?"

"These are just little keepsakes to remind me of the pleasant hours I spent here as the High Lama," I said. "I mean, it ain't as if you got any picture postcards I can take with me."

"The amulet," he said, holding out his hand.

Well, his other hand was perched on the handle of his sword, so I sighed and took it off from around my neck and tossed it onto the bed.

Then I followed him down to the main level of the temple, out the door, across the fields, and over to the bridge. All the guards took one look at me and immediately knelt down and bowed their heads, and I was across the bridge before anyone looked up. They hooted and hollered a lot, but I knew none of 'em would cross the stream to come after me as long as doing so would qualify 'em for a quick trip to the old age home.

As I headed toward India, I decided that the Land of Eternal Youth wasn't all it was cracked up to be, especially since it seemed to go hand-in-glove with eternal poverty, and I redirected all my more serious contemplating toward rounding up a grubstake and building the Tabernacle of St. Luke.

7. SECRET SEX

There are worse things than walking down the streets of Delhi on a hot summer day.

For one thing, you could be walking down the streets of Delhi on a hot summer day with a bunch of knife-wielding gamblers hot on your trail for trying to pay off your losses with a pandaskin coat.

Or you could be walking down the streets of Delhi on a hot summer day with half the British Raj hunting for you because you figured that white men ought to stick together in foreign climes and you borrowed a few thousand rupees from the local church and left an IOU in its place so that you could pay off all them disgruntled gamblers.

Or you could be walking down the streets of Delhi on a hot summer day with the Royal Governor's private guards searching for you after you figured you'd raise a little capital by selling tours to the executive mansion to a group of British clergymen, and when you got a mite confused and turned right instead of left, you came across the Royal Governor and a pair of chambermaids reenacting a solemn Biblical scene what probably took place on a regular basis between Solomon and a couple of his more athletic wives.

Or you could be walking down the streets of Delhi looking out for the father and eight burly brothers of one of the city's fairest flowers, who in their enthusiasm to welcome a little fresh blood into the family seemed totally unable to differentiate between a declaration of eternal love and a bonafide proposal of marriage.

All of which had happened to me through a series of innocent misunderstandings, but which nonetheless imbued me with a pretty strong desire to take my leave of Delhi until everyone calmed down and was willing to listen to reason.

It was when I saw a handful of the Royal Governor's men standing in the middle of the road, comparing notes with a couple of gamblers, that I decided it might be a good idea to duck into a nearby building and wait for nightfall before clearing out, so I walked through the nearest door and found myself in the lobby of the Victoria Hotel, which looked like it had been sadly in need of a spring cleaning for the better part of half a century or so.

"May I help you, Sahib?" asked the desk clerk, who was a skinny little Indian with a dirty turban.

"Yeah," I said, looking out the window as the governor's men started looking into all the shops and stores. "I need a place to stay, kind of short term."

"We have a number of empty rooms," he said.

"I don't need nothing for the whole night," I said. "Five or ten minutes should do the trick."

He frowned. "We have never rented a room for less than the night, Sahib," he said.

"I ain't got no time to haggle," I said, flashing my last fifty rupees and walking around behind the desk next to him. "I'll just rent this here floor space for half an hour. Payable when I get up and leave."

I sat down about ten seconds before a couple of soldiers entered the lobby and walked over to the clerk.

"We're looking for an American masquerading as a minister," said one of them. "Have you seen him?"

I shoved half the rupees into the clerk's hand.

"No, Sahibs," he answered. "No one has come in here all day."

"Well, if he should, let us know."

"Certainly, Sahibs," he said.

He waited until they walked out and closed the door behind them, then turned and looked down at me.

"You can stand up now," he said. "They're gone."

"It's kind of comfortable down here," I said. "Besides, they were just the first wave of an unending ocean of misfortune."

"There are more people looking for you?" he asked.

"No more'n eighty or ninety of 'em," I answered.

"What did you do?"

"Hardly anything at all," I said. "These English fellers just can't stand the fact that we whipped 'em at Bunker Hill. All I can figure is that they're still carrying a grudge."

"I hate the English, too," he said. "Even now we are planning to drive them from our country as you Americans did."

"You don't say?"

"I do say," he replied. He paused and stared at me for a minute or two. "Would I be correct in assuming you plan to leave Delhi when night falls?"

"I got to admit that sticking around waiting to get tarred and feathered ain't real high on my list of priorities," I answered.

"They will be watching all the major roads and train stations," he said. "If you try to get out by foot or car or train, they will stop you."

"That's right depressing news," I said.

"But I can get you out," he added.

"Well, as one revolutionary to another, let me say that that's mighty neighborly of you."

"I will be happy to help you thwart the British," he said. "And once you are safely away from Delhi, I hope you will do me a favor in return."

"Doing favors for ignorant brown heathen is part of my calling," I assured him. "No offense intended."

"None taken."

"Exactly what kind of favor did you have in mind?"

"I will tell you when the time comes," he said, handing me a room key. "In the meantime, I have arrangements to make. Wait for me in this room. I will knock three times at midnight."

"Sounds good to me," I said, getting up onto my feet. "By the way, I never did catch your name."

"Gunga, and no bad jokes, please."

"Why would I make a joke, Brother Gunga?" I asked.

"The British seem to find it hilarious," he said bitterly.

"It don't bother me none," I said.

"I take it you don't like Kipling?"

"It ain't never been one of my favorite sports," I replied. "And by the bye, I'm the Right Reverend Honorable Doctor Lucifer Jones, at your service."

"You'd better get to your room now, before anyone else comes looking for you," suggested Gunga.

Well, I did like he said, and spent a few minutes finding solace for my present situation in the Good Book before I drifted off to sleep. I must have been tireder than I thought, because the next thing I knew Gunga was knocking at the door.

"Are you ready, Sahib?" he whispered.

"Ready and rarin'," I said, opening the door.

"Everything has been prepared," he said, walking into the room.

"Sounds good to me," I said. "How am I getting out—by car or by train?"

"Neither," he answered. "Take off your clothes."

"I can hardly blame you for being smitten by my manly good looks," I said sternly, "but us men of the cloth don't go in for no degenerate activity."

"Get into this," he said, tossing me a white loincloth. "It's part of your disguise."

Now that I knew he wasn't gonna attempt no unnatural perversions, I got undressed right quick and clambered into the loincloth. Then he walked over and tied a turban around my head.

"How do I look?" I asked.

He studied me thoughtfully for a moment. "Like an American in a loincloth and turban," he said. "Still, it will have to do. Follow me, please."

He walked out the door and down the stairs, with me right behind him, and then we went through the kitchen and out the back door, where I bumped smack-dab into an elephant.

"Say hello to Akbar," said Gunga. "He will take you out of Delhi."

"I don't know how to tell you this, Brother Gunga," I said, staring at Akbar, of whom there was an awful lot to stare at, "but I ain't never rode no elephants before."

"The British will never be looking for a coolie atop an elephant," said Gunga. "You should pass by unnoticed."

"That's a powerful lot of elephant to pass by anything unnoticed," I said.

"Trust me, Reverend Jones," said Gunga. "It is your only chance."

"You I trust," I said. "Akbar I got my doubts about."

"He is trained to respond to whoever is his mahout."

"His what?"

"His rider," said Gunga. He handed me a stick with a metal hook at one end. "To make him go, just say 'Kush.' Use the stick to turn him." He looked up and down the alleyway. "I must leave shortly."

"How do I get on top of him?"

"Just stand in front of him and tell him to lift you up."

"That's all there is to it?" I asked dubiously.

"Trust me, Reverend Jones."

"Well, I suppose I ought to thank you for going to all this trouble, Brother Gunga," I said.

"You can repay a favor with a favor," he replied.

"Just name it," I said, keeping my fingers crossed behind my back in case it involved giving money to one of his pet charities.

"Take Akbar to the town of Khajuraho, which is south and east of here. Once you arrive there you will be contacted by our leader, Rashid Jahan." He looked around nervously. "Now I must leave before my absence is noticed."

He darted back into the hotel, and I was left alone with Akbar, who looked like he didn't trust me a whole lot more than I trusted him, which was not at all. Still, I couldn't just stand there in the alley forever, so I finally walked around to his front end and said "Lift." His trunk snaked out and wrapped itself around me, and before I could scream for help or ask my Silent Partner to intervene I was sitting on top of his head. I tucked a leg behind each ear, said "Kush!", and off old Akbar went. When we came to a corner I jabbed him with the stick, and sure enough, he turned just the way he was supposed to.

We made it to the edge of town in less than an hour, and the British soldiers just waved me past without even looking at me, and then we started kushing south. Akbar wasn't the type to travel on an empty stomach, and he ate on the march, so to speak, and by the time morning rolled around I decided that maybe he had the right idea about things, so I steered him to a nearby apple orchard and told him to stop, but evidently he didn't speak no American because he just kept on plodding along at the same brisk pace. I managed to grab a couple of apples off a low-hanging branch or I could have starved for all Akbar gave a damn.

About noon we hit a forest, and started plowing through it, and then suddenly old Akbar's trunk shot straight out and his ears stopped flopping and started listening, and a minute later he began trumpeting to beat the band, and just about the time I was sure he was trying to warn me that the Royal Governor was waiting in ambush I heard an answering trumpet and then a wild elephant broke into a clearing. I started whacking Akbar with my stick to make him turn around, because even though this wild elephant was a couple of feet smaller than him I still didn't relish sitting on his head while he indulged himself in a friendly little fight to the death, but he just kept walking forward, and at the last second I realized that the wild elephant was of the female persuasion and I was about to become an inadvertent participant in an affair of the heart.

Well, Akbar stopped when he was maybe two feet away and trumpeted again, and she trumpeted back, and pretty soon you could have sworn that a brass band was giving a concert of John Philip Sousa marches what with all the trumpeting that was going on. Then the lady elephant gave Akbar a playful shove that could have brought a house down, and Akbar started prancing around like a puppy, and then suddenly there was a great crashing of bushes and trees and another elephant broke into the clearing some forty yards away. This one was bigger than Akbar, and he had a jealous husbandly look about him, and Akbar right quick decided he had urgent business elsewhere, because he took off like a bat out of hell and didn't slow down until we reached the end of the forest and broke out into the open once again.

Losing the love of his life seemed to take all the zip out of Akbar's stride, but it didn't affect his appetite none, so he munched and plodded his way across the countryside for the rest of the day and all the next night.

It was dawn when we hit the outskirts of Khajuraho, and the first thing I saw was this temple, which wasn't like no other I had ever seen, and truth to tell reminded me a lot more of the Rialto Burlesque Theater back in Kansas City than a house of worship. There were a bunch of figures, carved as big as life, all over the walls of the temple, most of 'em dressed for extremely warm weather, and all of them doing exactly what Akbar had planned to do with his lady elephant.

We went a little farther, and came to another temple with even more enthusiastic figures on the walls, and by the time we hit a third temple that was just like the first two only more so, I figured I had finally found the perfect community to build my tabernacle.

I turned Akbar toward town, and when we came to a rundown hostelry called the Janata Hotel, I pointed him toward a brick wall since I didn't know no other way to stop him, and while he was pushing against it I took a stroll down the middle of his back and slid off when I came to his tail. Then I walked around to the front and told the desk clerk to give me a room with a bath, and tend to my elephant for me.

"I'm sorry," he said, staring at me, "but we do not cater to the native trade."

Which was when I remembered that I was all done up like a coolie.

"Don't pay no nevermind to these duds," I said. "I was just out getting a suntan."

"You sound like an American," he said. "I thought only we British ran around naked in the midday sun in tropical climes."

"I ain't so much running around as trying to rent a room," I pointed out.

He got out the register right quick, and I signed in, and a few minutes later I was sitting in my bathtub washing off the smell of elephant, of which I'd acquired an awful lot, when there was a knock at the door.

"Come on in," I hollered. "It ain't locked."

A little Indian feller walked into the room and headed over to the tub.

"You are Lucifer Jones?" he asked.

"The Right Reverend Honorable Doctor Lucifer Jones, at your service," I said.

"I have been waiting for you ever since I got a telegram from my cousin Gunga," he said. "I am Rashid Jahan."

"You hunted me up kind of fast, Brother Rashid," I remarked.

"Well, we knew we were looking for a white man wearing a loincloth and riding an elephant," he replied. "You'd be surprised how very few of them come through town in a day."

"So what can I do for you, Brother Rashid?"

"I understand from my cousin Gunga that the two of you discussed expelling the British from our country."

"Yeah, I recall his mentioning something about it," I said.

"And I further understand that you share our philosophy."

Now, I couldn't figure out how Gunga had known that, since I hadn't seen any of the temples until I hit Khajuraho, but I allowed that he was dead right.

"Excellent!" said Rashid. "He also mentioned that you had promised to do us a favor in exchange for his help."

"True enough," I said.

"Then I wonder if you would be willing to visit our secret sex tonight?" he said.

"Your secret sex?" I said.

He nodded. "We could draw enormous inspiration from an American like yourself."

I thought for a moment about the temples I had passed by on my way into town, and I figured that if that was their notion of public sex, I couldn't wait to see what kind of secret sex they practiced.

"I consider it a debt of honor, Brother Rashid," I said. "I'll inspire the hell out of 'em."

"Excellent," he said. "I shall tell them that you will join us."

"As often and as vigorously as I can," I promised. "Where do I find this here secret sex?"

"Wait until ten o'clock tonight, and then come south of town to the Temple of Kali."

"I'll be there with bells on," I assured him.

He bowed and left, and I spent the next couple of hours just soaking in the tub. Then, just after sunset, I got out and changed into my best Sunday go-to-meeting clothes, after which I shaved and slapped a bunch of grease on my hair to slick it down. I didn't have no file to clean the dirt out from under my fingernails, so I bit 'em off instead. I didn't have any cologne neither, so I wandered down to the bar and slapped a little Napoleon brandy on my face when the barkeep wasn't looking.

Then, since I had high hopes of meeting a lady of quality at this secret sex affair, I moseyed out into the hotel's garden and picked a couple of dozen flowers which I wrapped in a copy of the *Bombay Times* that someone had left in the lobby.

Finally I went looking for Akbar, and found him munching peacefully on some greenery down the street.

"Lift," I said, and he did, and soon we were heading down the road to the Temple of Kali. I still hadn't figured out how to make him stop, so I just aimed him up against a huge pillar, and while he was pushing away at it I climbed down and walked around to the front door, holding the flowers behind my back since I didn't want to give 'em to the first lady I saw, just in case a prettier one was hanging back just waiting for a handsome young buck like me to sweep her off her feet.

I knocked on the door, and Rashid opened it.

"You're right on time, Reverend Jones," he said.

"Well, I didn't want no one to start without me," I said. "Which way to the secret sex?"

"Follow me," he said, walking me past a couple of dozen statues that looked so acrobatic that the models could probably have gotten jobs with the Ringling Brothers if they'd put their clothes on.

We took a hard left, and then went down a flight of stairs to this big ornate door, where Rashid stopped and turned to me.

"You are a Westerner," he said, "unused to our ways. I warn you that you may be shocked by some of the things that you will see before the evening is over."

"Different strokes for different folks," I said.

"I admire your open-mindedness, Reverend Jones."

He reached out for the door and was just about to open it when a figure darted out of the shadows and cracked him over the head with a blackjack, and he just kind of smiled and blinked once or twice and then collapsed on the floor.

"Reverend Jones!" whispered the figure, which was dressed all in black. "What in blazes are *you* doing here?"

I turned to face him, and realized that I was looking at Sir Mortimer Edgerton-Smythe.

"Howdy, Sir Mortimer," I said. "Last time I saw you you were heading into the sunset with Dr. Aristotle Ho's dragon. What happened?"

"That foul fiend duped me," said Sir Mortimer. "But now I've gotten wind of his latest plot to take over the world, and I plan to bring him to justice."

"And you figure hitting my friend Rashid on the noggin is going to have a deleterious effect on a Chinaman who's four thousand miles away from here?" I asked.

"I did it to save *you*, Reverend Jones," he said. "Now I must have an answer to my question: what are you doing here?"

"I been invited to participate in some secret sex," I said. "And while I don't mean to be critical or nothing, you're putting a real damper on the festivities."

"You fool!" he snapped. "You have no idea what's going on behind that door!"

"I'm a quick study," I assured him.

"You're totally unprepared for this."

I considered what he said and looked down at my flowers. "You think I should have brung candy instead?"

"You shouldn't have come at all," he said. "Take my advice and go right back to your hotel."

"Now just a minute, Sir Mortimer," I said. "I'm glad to share some of this here secret sex with you, you being a fellow white man and all, but I'll be hanged if I'm gonna leave and let you have it all to yourself."

"What's going on behind that door is a meeting of secret *sects*, you blithering idiot!" he said.

"Secret sects?" I repeated.

"Dr. Aristotle Ho has resurrected the Thuggees and other ancient sects with the purpose of overrunning India and eventually all of Asia, with himself as their leader. Tonight is the night that they have all gathered under one roof so that he can address them and spell out his plans. *Now* do you understand what you have blundered into?"

"You mean there ain't no women in there?" I asked.

"That's what I've been trying to tell you!"

"And I got all decked out in my Sunday best for nothing?"

"Don't you understand anything I've said?" demanded Sir Mortimer.

"I understand that Dr. Aristotle Ho has got a lot to answer for," I told him. "This was a downright cruel and unfeeling trick to play on a Christian missionary who never did nobody no harm."

Sir Mortimer stared at me for a minute. "I don't suppose it matters what your motive is, as long as you're against him. What do you say, Reverend Jones—will you throw in with me and bring this insidious villain to justice?"

"I should consider my answer very carefully before I gave it, Doctor Jones," said a familiar voice, and we turned to find ourselves facing Doctor Aristotle Ho and maybe a dozen of his henchmen, all of 'em with their guns drawn.

"*You!*" hissed Sir Mortimer.

"Our paths cross once again, Sir Mortimer," said Doctor Ho. "You are becoming a serious annoyance to me. I should have killed you the last time we met; this time I will correct that oversight."

"Well, I can see you two have lots to talk about," I said, "so if you'll excuse me, I think I'll be on my way."

"Not so fast, Doctor Jones," he said, as a couple of his men blocked my path. "Why are you here in the first place?"

"It's a Saturday night, and I was looking for a little female companionship," I explained.

"At a meeting of the Thuggees in the Temple of Kali?" he said, kind of arching an eyebrow.

"I was the victim of false doctrine," I said. "Everybody kept talking about all this secret sex that was going on, and I thought I'd partake of some of it."

He stared at me for an awfully long and uncomfortable minute.

"Nobody can be that foolish, Doctor Jones," he said. "Not even you. Therefore, I must conclude that you are working in concert with Sir Mortimer."

"I didn't even know he was gonna be here!" I protested. "I even brung these flowers along for the lucky lady of my choice."

"An excellent disguise," said Doctor Ho, nodding approvingly. "Who would suspect such a naive, bumbling idiot of being a master spy?"

"I ain't no master spy," I said. "I'm just an innocent man of the cloth, bringing spiritual comfort across the face of Asia to all you unwashed heathen."

"Please do not insult my intelligence, Doctor Jones," said Aristotle Ho. "Do you think I am unaware of your exploits since last we met? You killed one of my most trusted agents, General Chang, in hand-to-hand combat atop the Great Wall, and then made off with *my* jade." He paused and glared at me. "You fooled me the first time we met, but now I know just how dangerous you are."

"Sir Mortimer," I said, "tell him I ain't working for you!"

"You know, you fooled me too, Doctor Jones," said Sir Mortimer admiringly. "Who *are* you working for—the United States government or some private organization of super assassins?"

"Thanks a heap, Sir Mortimer," I said glumly.

"Enough talking," said Doctor Ho. "Now you shall see what happens to those who are foolish enough to attempt to hinder me in my goal of world conquest! Open the door!"

One of his henchmen pulled the door open, and we marched into this huge chamber that had about three hundred men in it, all of 'em wearing red robes with weird designs on 'em. A couple of men were laying on stone altars, but since their heads were missing I figured they weren't in any real serious pain at the moment. The second the guys wearing the robes saw us they pulled out their swords and knives, but then Doctor Ho raised his hand and everyone stood stock-still.

"I have captured these two spies," he announced. "What shall we do with them?"

Well, just about everyone in the room screamed "Death!", but I did hear one voice say "Let's rape them first!", which implied to me that at least one other person had come looking for a little secret sex himself.

"How shall we kill them?" demanded Doctor Ho.

"The Death of a Thousand Cuts!" yelled a batch of 'em.

"Do you know what the Death of a Thousand Cuts is?" Doctor Ho said to me.

"Sounds like trying to shave with a hangover," I opined.

"I am afraid not, Doctor Jones," he said. "First, we will string you up and hang you a few feet above the floor. Then we will start slicing you to ribbons, but we will not deliver the fatal blow until the thousandth cut. The pain will be exquisite, I assure you."

"I got a better idea," I said. "If you really want to string this out, why not give me one cut tonight? Then I could go back to my hotel and sleep it off, and I promise to show up each of the next nine hundred and ninety-nine nights."

"What kind of fool do you take me for?" demanded Doctor Ho.

"Do your worst!" bellowed Sir Mortimer. "I will show you how an Englishman dies."

Well, I wasn't right anxious to show *anyone* how an American died, so I turned back to Doctor Ho again.

"This is silly," I said to him. "I ain't no spy, and you probably ain't got no followers what can count all the way up to a thousand. Why don't we just shake hands and let bygones be bygones? I'll even buy you a drink back at the Janata Hotel."

"You have heard the verdict of my Thuggees," replied Doctor Ho sternly. "They demand blood."

"As long as Sir Mortimer seems bound and determined to bleed, why not settle for him?" I suggested. "I'll even do some of the cutting, just as a gesture of Christian goodwill."

"I admire your coolness in the face of an excruciatingly painful death, Doctor Jones," said Aristotle Ho. "Under other circumstances we could have been great friends."

"It still ain't too late," I said. "I feel a burst of friendship coming over me right this second."

He shook his head. "You are much too dangerous to be allowed to live." He turned to his men. "Prepare them both for the Death of a Thousand Cuts."

"Remember," said Sir Mortimer, as they dragged us to the center of the room, "we represent the civilized world. Don't give them the pleasure of screaming in agony no matter how terrible the pain. Keep a stiff upper lip."

I was about to point out the difficulty of keeping a stiff upper lip once they chopped if off, but by then we were surrounded by Thuggees who placed us on a large platform and ripped our jackets and shirts off and started to tie our hands behind our backs when Doctor Ho stepped forward again.

"One moment," he said, and everything came to a stop. "I know you think me a barbaric fiend, Sir Mortimer," he continued, "but actually I am one of the more civilized fiends I know. To that end, I will allow you to make a last statement, if you so desire."

Sir Mortimer was already getting into his impersonation of the strong, silent type, and he just glared at Doctor Ho without saying a word.

"Doctor Jones?" said Aristotle Ho. "Have you any last words?"

I looked up toward the ceiling. "Lord," I said, "pay attention now: this is Your friend and admirer Lucifer Jones suggesting that if You ever plan to manifest Yourself, You couldn't pick a much more opportune time than this here moment to bring the temple crumbling down."

Doctor Ho threw back his head to laugh, but before a sound had a chance to come out we heard a great crashing noise and the whole temple started shaking. A couple of seconds later the ceiling started caving in, and half the Thuggees were buried under it while the rest lit out for the hills with a speed and grace that would have done Jim Thorpe proud.

Suddenly there was no one left except me and Sir Mortimer and Aristotle Ho, and he just glared at us furiously for a second, and then said, "You have thwarted me today, Lucifer Jones, but you haven't heard the last of me!" And then, before we could say anything, he melted into the shadows.

"Thanks a lot, Lord!" I shouted. "Now I owe *You* a favor!"

Then we heard a mournful trumpeting, and we raced up what remained of the stairs, and there was old Akbar beating his head against a wall of the temple. He'd been pushing against the pillar where I left him until it finally collapsed on top of the Thuggees' private meeting room, and since nobody had told him to stop he'd just proceeded forward a few feet until he came to the wall, which wasn't near as thick and was already starting to buckle.

"Well, Doctor Jones," said Sir Mortimer. "Once again we've put a crimp in that insidious fiend's plan to conquer the world! Well done, sir!"

"Well, that's what he gets for leading an innocent gentleman on with promises of secret sex," I said righteously.

"I must be on my way, to report the night's proceedings to my government," he said. "It was nice collaborating with you again." He paused. "Allow me to give you one last piece of advice: do not return to your hotel tonight. There's always a chance that Aristotle Ho will be waiting there for you."

Well, I hadn't planned on returning anyway, since there was a dead certainty that the desk clerk and the hotel manager would be waiting there for me, and I had a feeling that they wouldn't accept payment in elephants, so I bade Sir Mortimer good-bye, got atop old Akbar again, and making a vow not to be duped by Doctor Aristotle Ho ever again, I headed off in search of fame, fortune, and maybe a little public sex with an obliging lady of quality.

8. THE FLAME OF BHARATPUR

Twenty-five rupees didn't buy a lot of food, even back in 1930, so Akbar and I kept pretty much to the countryside, eating whatever we could find in the fields, and heading in a kind of westerly direction. After a couple of weeks we hit the Rajasthan province, and the landscape got a little prettier, and we started passing an occasional old temple, and here and there we came to deserted cities, but since I still didn't know how to make him come to a stop I didn't get no chance to examine them.

It was when we were nearing Jaipur, where I had every hope of finding a used elephant lot and trading old Akbar in for a grubstake and maybe finding a friendly little game of chance, that we came across a field of tall grasses backing up to a forest. I was about to head for the trees in the hope that some of 'em might have something nourishing hanging down from their branches when I saw a movement in the grass off to my left, and I heard this voice whispering "Help me!", so I steered Akbar in that direction.

Then, when we were about twenty yards away, I heard a great big "*Oof!*" kind of sound, like something had had all the air squoze out of it, so I jumped off Akbar to see what was the matter, and what I found was that he had accidentally stepped on this tiger and crushed it flatter than a board.

I walked over to where the voice had come from, and found a white man, all torn up and bleeding, lying in the grass.

"Thank God!" he whispered when he saw me.

"What seems to be the problem, Brother?" I asked, kneeling down next to him.

Well, he was kind of delirious, and he kept mumbling about a tiger hunt and jealous lovers and murder and some kind of flame or fire, and finally I figured I'd better get him to a doctor right quick, so I called Akbar over and told him to lift us up, and once I laid the man across Akbar's neck and perched myself on his head, we made tracks for Jaipur, where we went to the nearest hospital. I left Akbar pushing his head against the wall of the emergency room, while I turned the patient over to a couple of doctors who carted him off and went right to work on him. I decided to hang around for awhile, inasmuch as I didn't have no place better to go anyway, and before long I made fast friends with a pretty little nurse who rustled up some hospital grub for me, and then after a couple of hours one of the doctors hunted me up to say that the patient was going to live and wanted to see me, and not to do anything to wear him out, as if he was expecting me to arm-wrestle him or something.

I entered the room and walked over to the bed, where the fellow I had saved was all covered in bandages.

"I'm told that I owe you my life," he said weakly.

"All in a day's work," I said, "me being a servant of the Lord and all."

"Well, your intervention was divinely inspired," he said. He reached out a hand to me. "My name is Geoffrey Bainbridge."

"The Right Reverend Doctor Lucifer Jones, at your service," I replied, taking his hand kind of gingerly. "Just out of idle curiosity, Brother Bainbridge, what in tarnation were you doing, alone and unarmed, in tiger country?"

"It's a complicated tale of desire and deceit, Doctor Jones," he said.

"That's my very favorite kind of tale, Brother Bainbridge," I said. "Take all the desire and deceit out of the Good Book and you wouldn't have more than a handful of chapters left."

"It all revolves around the Flame of Bharatpur," he said.

"Yeah?"

"Maybe I should begin at the beginning," he said. "I'm a bachelor, Doctor Jones. Some months ago, while judging a livestock show, I made the acquaintance of Lady Edith Quilton, the widow of Lord Randolph Quilton, who owns the largest estate in all of Rajasthan. We struck up a friendship, and shared many an afternoon tea together, and finally I proposed marriage to her." He paused. "I shall be perfectly honest with you, Doctor Jones. While I enjoy her company and admire her adventurous spirit, the real reason I wanted to marry her was to gain possession of the Flame of Bharatpur."

"I take it this Flame of Bharatpur is worth a bundle of money?" I said.

"The Flame of Bharatpur is perfection itself," he said. Suddenly he frowned. "But even as I was pressing my suit, another gentleman entered her life."

"He wanted the Flame of Bharatpur too?" I asked.

"He wants everything she owns," replied Bainbridge. "She is quite the wealthiest woman in the province, and he is a low, deceitful fortune hunter."

Well, truth to tell, I couldn't see much difference between a selective fortune hunter and a generalized one, but I just sat there and listened to Bainbridge pour out his story.

"We disliked one another at first sight, although we continued to behave in a civilized manner toward each other. But things reached a head this morning. Lady Edith organized a tiger hunt, and I found myself sharing a howdah with this villain. Feigning enthusiasm, he drove our elephant far ahead of the others, and when the beaters flushed a tiger, he grabbed my rifle and pushed me out of the howdah, racing off and leaving me to face the tiger's charge unarmed and on foot. The brute knocked me down and raked me with its claws, and was about to finish me off when you providentially arrived." He leaned his head back against the pillow, all wore out from telling his story. "And now, although I owe my life to you and can never repay you, I must nevertheless ask you one last favor, Doctor Jones."

"What did you have in mind, Brother Bainbridge?" I asked, just kind of figuring to humor him until he drifted off to sleep.

"I realize that it was wrong of me to propose a loveless marriage simply to gain possession of the Flame of Bharatpur," he said. "But I cannot leave poor Edith to the mercies of her current suitor, and I will be in no condition to confront him for weeks or possibly even months. *You* must prevent that filthy fortune hunter from possessing the Flame of Bharatpur, even if it means marrying her yourself."

"Well, now, that's a right interesting proposition, Brother Bainbridge," I said. "And now that I come to mull on it, I can see that it's my Christian duty to save this poor woman from such a scoundrel, even if it means I got to spend the rest of my life helping her manage her fortune rather than bringing the word of the Lord to these poor deprived brown heathen."

"Then you'll do it?" he said.

"Brother Bainbridge," I said, "it's as good as done."

"You are truly one of nature's noblemen," he said, and suddenly he was sound asleep, and I kind of tiptoed out of his room before he could wake up and change his mind, and a couple of minutes later me and Akbar were headed off to Lady Edith's estate on the edge of town.

I didn't know her exact address, but when I came to a house that was just a little bit smaller than Buckingham Palace and had even nicer gardens, I knew I'd hit paydirt, so to speak. I figured Akbar might prove to be a bit of a social handicap, especially since he'd recently developed a taste for flowers, so I pointed him down the road, wished him well, and took my leave of him. Last I saw of him he was just vanishing over the top of a small hill, and with no one to tell him to stop, I figured he'd keep going until he hit the Indian Ocean, by which time he could probably use a little seaside vacation.

Then I wandered up the long, winding driveway and knocked on the front door. A couple of Indians, dressed all in white, let me in, and one of them escorted me to the drawing room while the other went and fetched Lady Edith. While I was waiting for her I decided to take a look around and see just what I was marrying into. I knew right off that Lady Edith liked the ballet, because there were a bunch of paintings of ballerinas hanging on the wall, all done by some Frenchman, and I could see that her late husband had an eye for the ladies, because there were also a few paintings of half-naked island girls by yet another Frenchman, which were so racy I would have thought she'd toss 'em out once her husband departed this mortal coil, but I couldn't see no signs of conspicuous wealth until I noticed a little glass case in the corner. I walked over to it and there, setting on a little gold pedestal, was the biggest, reddest ruby I ever did see, and I knew right off that this had to be the Flame of Bharatpur that all the fuss was about.

I heard a little feminine cough behind me, and turned to find myself facing a vigorous-looking woman of about fifty years. She was decked out in riding togs, and she held a leather crop in her hand.

"Just admiring your taste in gemstones, ma'am," I said. "You must be Lady Edith."

"I am afraid you have the advantage of me, Mr. ...?"

"Reverend, ma'am," I said. "The Right Reverend Doctor Lucifer Jones at your service, fresh from risking life and limb to save Geoffrey Bainbridge from a tiger attack."

"My goodness!" she said. "Is he all right?"

"The doctors say he'll be up and around in a couple of months," I said.

"How did it happen?"

"Well, it's a long story, ma'am, and being the modest Christian gentleman that I am I hate to set myself up as a fearless hero what dragged poor Geoffrey from the jaws of death and dispatched a tiger with my bare hands, so it's probably best left untold." I paused. "I do bring a message from him, though."

"What is it?" she asked.

"Due to the delicate nature of one of his injuries, he regrets to inform you that he's no longer on the marriage market, and he hopes you'll understand and won't think no less of him for it."

"The poor man!" she said. "We wondered what happened to him when he didn't show up for lunch after the hunt."

"He was probably preoccupied with bleeding to death at the time," I said. "It was just a stroke of providence that I came by when I did."

"You must tell me all about it," she said.

"Well, I'd enjoy doing so, Lady Edith, but Geoffrey ain't the only one what missed out on lunch, and I think now that I've delivered his tragic message to you, I'd best be getting back to town to hunt up some dinner."

"Nonsense," she said. "You will have dinner here, with us, Reverend Jones. It's the very least I can do for such a noble and courageous man."

"Well, I'd surely like to, Lady Edith," I said, "but I also ain't got no place to stay, and I'd better scare me up a room before all the hotels are sold out for the night."

"I won't hear of it," she said. "I'll have my servants make up a room for you right now."

"I couldn't impose on you like that, ma'am," I protested. "Even though I give all my money to the poor, I usually hold enough back to rent a cot in some flophouse."

"You're staying here, and that's all there is to it," she said firmly.

Well, I spent a couple of more minutes letting her argue me into it, and then I went up to my room and freshened up a bit. When my stomach told me that it was dinnertime, I opened the door and started walking down the hall to the big winding staircase that led to the main floor and the dining room, when I bumped into a familiar-looking figure coming out of his own room.

"Doctor Jones!" said Rupert Cornwall. "What the hell are you doing here?"

"Howdy, Brother Rupert," I greeted him. "You still on the run from Inspector Willie Wong?"

He put a finger to his lips. "I must ask you to be more discreet," he said, which I took to be an affirmative.

"No problem at all, Brother Rupert," I said. "But just out of curiosity, what's Hong Kong's most notorious criminal kingpin doing hiding out in Lady Edith's house?"

He grabbed me by the shoulder and pulled me into his room, then closed the door behind us. "I'm not hiding out, Doctor Jones," he said. "In point of fact, I'm here to press my suit upon her."

"Sounds painful," I said. "Wouldn't an ironing board do just as well?"

"You misunderstand," said Rupert. "I'm courting Lady Edith."

"So *you're* the guy who pushed Geoffrey Bainbridge out of the howdah," I said.

"How did you know that?" he demanded.

"I happened along just in time to save him from getting et by a tiger."

"You mean he's here right now?" asked Rupert, a kind of wild look about his eyes.

"No, he'll be indisposed for the next couple of months."

Rupert kind of chuckled at that. "Good!" he said. "I'll have her married long before then."

"Well, now, I sure wouldn't count on it, Brother Rupert," I said.

He stared at me kind of suspiciously. "Why not?"

"You might say that another player just entered the game," I answered.

"You?" he sneered. "You haven't got a chance with her."

"Well, that remains to be seen, don't it?" I said.

"I want you to know that I resent your intrusion, Doctor Jones," he said. "I'm the one who found this set-up. I think it's very unfair of you to come along now and try to horn in after I've laid all the romantic groundwork."

"Before you get to feeling too righteous, Brother Rupert," I said, "let me remind you that I'd still be in Hong Kong spending our ill-gotten gains if some criminal kingpin had played square with me."

"That was just business," he said innocently. "Surely a man of the world like yourself doesn't hold that against me."

"*This* is just business too, Brother Rupert," I said. "I'll make you a deal, though: I won't tell her how and where we met if you don't."

"I agree," he said. "And may the best man win."

"Especially if he's a handsome, God-fearing Christian missionary," I added.

We left his room then and went down the stairs to dinner, where we were joined by Lady Edith and maybe a dozen other house guests, most of them titled and all of them very old and very British. Afterward I recounted how I had pulled this raging tiger off poor Geoffrey Bainbridge's torn and tattered body and choked the life out of it, and when Lady Edith insisted that I stay over for a week or two, I shot Rupert a triumphant grin and figured that the Flame of Bharatpur was as good as mine.

We were up bright and early the next morning, and Lady Edith offered to show me around the place. She was dressed in her walking britches, and looking vigorous as all get-out, and she set a mighty fast pace, pointing out all her various flowers that had won prizes in flower shows. Then we visited the stables, and I saw her prize-winning horses, and after that we went to the kennels, where I saw her prize-winning dogs, and by the time we got to the barn to look at her prize-winning cattle and her prize-winning pigs I began to get the impression that Lady Edith was more than a little bit on the competitive side.

"I show them all over the continent," she said, pointing to a pair of bulls who were snorting to beat the band and looked like they wanted nothing more than a matador breakfast. "This one even took a first in England last year before I imported him."

One of the pigs started squealing, and she walked over and petted him. "This is Sylvester, my pride and joy," she confided to me. "He's won prizes in five different countries."

Well, I looked at Sylvester, and Sylvester looked at me, and all I could think was that he'd go mighty well with fried eggs and maybe some hash-brown potatoes, but I didn't want to offend Lady Edith, so I allowed that Sylvester was about the prettiest pig I'd ever seen. That seemed to satisfy her, and we moved along past the ducks and the chickens, most of which had blue ribbons tacked up next to their coops, and finally we finished the tour and returned to the house. "It's such a lovely day, why don't we have breakfast on the terrace?" she suggested.

Well, that suited me fine, since it meant I wouldn't have to share her company with my rival, and I followed her to a glass table with an umbrella over it. We sat down, and a couple of servants appeared from nowhere to serve us tea and little biscuits, and then they vanished again, and just as I was trying to figure out the best way to start charming her, she turned to me and reached her hand out for mine.

"I'm so glad you decided to stay, Lucifer," she said.

Well, I'd had ladies fall in love with me before, but never quite that fast, and I figured this was going to be even easier than I'd thought.

"Well, that's perfectly understandable, you being the vigorous and attractive woman you are, in the prime of life so to speak, and me being a dashing Christian gentleman of noble mind and bold spirit."

"You are the answer to my prayers," she continued.

"Yeah?" I said, wondering whether to pop the question now or wait a respectable amount of time, like maybe another five minutes. "Tell me about 'em."

"I've been so worried, what with all the tigers in the area," she said.

"Tigers?" I said, surprised. "Who in tarnation is talking about tigers?"

"We are," she replied. "That's why I'm so thrilled that you're here, Lucifer. As long as there are tigers in the area, all of my prize livestock is at risk, and to be perfectly honest, Mr. Cornwall, while a fine and thoughtful gentleman, really isn't the sort to comb the countryside looking for tigers—whereas you, the man who killed the tiger that attacked Geoffrey Bainbridge with your bare hands…"

"Well, it wasn't quite with my bare hands," I interrupted her uneasily.

"Don't be so modest, Lucifer," she said. "One of the local natives found and skinned the tiger, and the shopkeeper who bought the pelt said that there wasn't a bullet hole or even a knife wound anywhere on it." She paused and stared at me. "Will you agree to lead a tiger hunt this afternoon?"

"I'd sure like to, ma'am," I said, "but usually I set afternoons aside for prayer and meditation, me being a man of the cloth and all."

"Couldn't you forego your meditation this one time, Lucifer?" she said. "You would have my undying gratitude."

Well, it wasn't quite the same as her undying love, but it was a step in the right direction, and besides, I suddenly had a notion of how to impress the bejabbers out of her and make Rupert Cornwall look feeble by comparison.

"Well, God is a pretty understanding critter," I said. "I suppose He wouldn't mind if I took an afternoon off to clear up your tiger problem."

"Thank you," she said with a great big smile.

"Of course, you understand that I don't make of point of rasslin' tigers hand-to-hand," I continued. "It takes too much time, and it's right hard on my clothes."

"We have all the guns you could possibly need," she assured me. "I can supply you with beaters, trackers, gunbearers, elephants, anything you want."

"Well, I thank you for the offer, ma'am," I said, "but I couldn't risk the lives of the very heathen that I came to India to save. No, I think it'd be best if I just go out alone and match my wits and skills with the fearsome beasts of the jungle."

"What a remarkable man you are, Lucifer!" she said. "I didn't know such brave, adventurous spirits still existed!"

"That's because you been associating with men like Rupert Cornwall too long," I said. "Nature ain't run totally out of noblemen just yet."

"You may just have a point, Lucifer," she said, and I figured that I had just pulled ahead of Rupert right then and there.

Well, I spent the rest of the morning loafing around, and by noontime most of Lady Edith's guests were up and around, and even Rupert wandered downstairs looking for a little grub, so we all had lunch together while Lady Edith told 'em what a brave and fearless deed I was about to do on her behalf, and I modestly explained that it wasn't nothing special and indeed was all part of a day's work for a Christian gentleman of high moral standards what was intent on serving his fellow man, or woman as the case happened to be.

Rupert just kept looking at me like I was crazy, but everyone else was right impressed, and when it came time for me to pick up a gun and head out the door, all of the guests came up and hugged me one by one, which was a most fortuitous thing since it enabled me to lift a couple of the old gentlemen's wallets. Once I got outside I pulled about five hundred pounds out of 'em, then went back and announced that I was feeling mighty lucky this afternoon and thought I'd probably better take some extra ammunition along. We all hugged each other again, which allowed me to replace the wallets, and then I was out the door and walking boldly into the wild fields that surrounded Lady Edith's estate.

I walked for nearly a mile, and when I was sure no one was following me I took a hard right and headed off to Jaipur. It took me the better part of an hour to get there, and once I arrived I went right up to the first Indian I saw on the street and asked him where the local taxidermist was. He pointed out a shop down the block, and I went over to it and opened the door.

"Good afternoon on you, Sahib," said a pudgy Indian with a neat little beard. "How may I be at your service?"

"I'm in the market for tiger skins," I said. "You got any for sale?"

"How many do you want?" he asked.

"I dunno," I replied. "How many have you got?"

"You come back and see," he said, escorting me through a door to his workshop.

Well, there were skins galore back there, everything from tigers to leopards to deer to what-have-you, along with a fair sampling of elephant tusks and rhinoceros horns. He pulled out a tigerskin rug and held it up for me.

"Very nice rug, very nice price, Sahib," he said. "Forty pounds."

"I don't want no rugs," I said. "Just skins."

He ran over to another pile and held up a skin. "Beautiful tiger skin, this one, Sahib. The notorious Maneater of Dindori. For you, twenty-five pounds."

"What about those over there?" I asked, pointing to a pile of skins that had flies buzzing around them.

He shook his head. "Oh, you do not want these, Sahib," he said. "I have not had time to prepare them yet. They just arrived this week."

"How many of 'em are there?" I asked.

"Seven."

"Tell you what," I said. "I'll take 'em all off your hands for fifty pounds apiece."

His jaw dropped so far I thought it was going to hit the floor. Then he gave me a great big smile and nodded his head.

"You drive a hard bargain, Sahib," he said. "But what is a poor shopkeeper to do?"

"I'll tell you what he's to do," I said.

"Sahib?" he said, looking kind of puzzled.

"For another hundred and fifty pounds, he's to keep his mouth shut about this little transaction."

For just a minute there I had the feeling that he was going to get down on his knees and kiss my feet, but he showed admirable restraint and a few minutes later I had loaded all seven skins into a cart he loaned me and started back toward Lady Edith's estate.

When I was maybe three miles away I made a big semi-circle and wound up in the fields where Akbar had accidentally saved Geoffrey Bainbridge's life the day before, and I took my rifle and fired seven quick shots into the air. Then I sat down and smoked a cigar, hid the cart in the woods, and started lugging the tiger skins up to Lady Edith's house.

Just about the time I hove into view a bunch of her servants ran out to greet me, screaming and cheering wildly, and took the skins from me, and then all the guests started yelling "Hip hip hooray!" and Lady Edith ran up and planted a great big kiss on me, and Rupert looked like if someone had given him a shovel he'd have dug a hole and crawled right into it.

About an hour later we all sat down for dinner, and I recounted the story about how I'd wiped out all the tigers in the neighborhood, adding a number of properly heroic embellishments, and Lady Edith couldn't take her eyes off me, and everyone kept asking me to tell it over and over again, and Rupert just sat and looked like something he'd et had disagreed kind of violently with him.

We adjourned to the drawing room, where I gave 'em a few last thrilling details of the hunt, and then they started heading off to their bedrooms, and Lady Edith gave me another kiss and shook Rupert's hand goodnight, and finally I didn't have no one left to tell my story to, so I went up to my room.

I hadn't been there more than a minute or two when Rupert came in and closed the door behind him.

"All right, Doctor Jones," he said. "I don't know how you did it, but you've managed to turn her head. Temporarily."

LUCIFER JONES VOLUME TWO: EXPLOITS

"Well, it's mighty decent of you to acknowledge that, Brother Rupert," I said.

"I didn't come here to flatter you," said Rupert. "I came here to talk business. What will it take to buy you off?"

"What makes you think I want to be bought off?" I asked.

"Why spend the rest of your life in a loveless marriage when I can make you independently wealthy?" he said.

"Ain't that what *you* plan to do?" I replied.

"That's beside the point," said Rupert. "Name your price."

"Okay," I said, after mulling on it for a minute or two. "I want the Flame of Bharatpur."

He looked at me kind of funny-like. "That's *it*?" he asked.

"Well, not quite," I said. "I hate farewell scenes with love-crazed women, so I'm going to leave tonight while everyone's asleep, and I want you to give her a note from me saying that I was called away because my wife is having a baby, which should help ease her sorrow. I'll take the Flame of Bharatpur with me on the way out."

"That's impossible," he said. "She has guards posted everywhere. There's no way you can take the Flame tonight without being caught out."

"Well," I said, "then I guess I'll just have to stick around and marry her."

"No, wait," said Rupert, lowering his head in thought for a minute. Finally he looked up. "I'll tell you what. Leave in the middle of the night like you planned, and go to Geoffrey Bainbridge's house. I'll remove the Flame of Bharatpur tomorrow when security isn't so tight, and have it delivered there before dark."

"I trust in human nature as much as any man," I said, "but I'd rest a mite easier if you'd write me a letter saying that you gave me the Flame of Bharatpur in exchange for ending my courtship of Lady Edith. Just in case something happens to the Flame in the meantime."

Well, he hemmed and he hawed, but finally he sat down and wrote the letter, and I jotted down a note to Lady Edith, and a few hours later I was walking down the road to the hospital, which I reached just after daylight. They didn't want to let Bainbridge out, but when I told him that the Flame of Bharatpur was being delivered to his house that day nothing they could say could make him stay there, and finally his chauffeur drove up and packed us into the car.

"I can't believe you got the Flame of Bharatpur in just one day!" said Bainbridge as we drove down the road toward his house.

"Well, it's our little secret," I said, after I'd told him the deal I'd made with Rupert Cornwall. "Lady Edith don't know nothing about it yet."

"I fully understand," he replied. "What I plan to do is keep the Flame against the day when she regains her senses and sends the rascal packing."

"That's all well and good for you," I said, "but what about me? After all, I'm the one who got Rupert to part with it."

"You will not go unrewarded, Doctor Jones."

"Good," I said. "Because I figure half of the Flame of Bharatpur belongs to me, and that probably translates into three or four million pounds on the open market."

He turned and stared at me. "Are you crazy?" he said.

"Okay," I said agreeably. "I forgot there's a depression on. I'll settle for a million."

We reached Bainbridge's house, and suddenly the car screeched to a halt just before it ran into a pig that was munching some flowers at the edge of the driveway.

"Looks like Rupert ain't been here yet," I said, but I suddenly found I was talking to an empty seat, because Geoffrey Bainbridge had gotten out of the car and was kneeling, bandages and all, next to the pig, running his hand lovingly over its head.

"Nice Sylvester," he was crooning. "Sweet Sylvester."

"You know," I said, climbing out of the car, "Lady Edith's got a pig called Sylvester that looks just like this one. Ain't that a striking coincidence?"

"This is him," said Bainbridge.

"Yeah? What's he doing here?"

"It means that Rupert Cornwall kept his word."

"What are you talking about?" I demanded.

"Sylvester," he said. "Champion The Flame of Bharatpur. He's won prizes in five different countries. Isn't he gorgeous?"

"The Flame of Bharatpur is a *pig*?"

"He's not merely a pig," said Bainbridge. "He is the greatest swine I have ever seen!"

Well, right at that moment I had my own opinions about the greatest swine I had ever seen, and Rupert Cornwall and Geoffrey Bainbridge were running neck-and-neck for the award. I couldn't go back and rekindle my romance with Lady Edith, because by now she'd read my note, and I didn't see Sylvester bringing no multi-million dollar price on the black market even if I could convince Bainbridge to part with him, and I'd spent every penny I had on tiger skins, so I decided then and there that I would take Bainbridge's reward and go to some country where folks wasn't so all-fired deceitful and an honest man of God could build a tabernacle and finally get around to doing some serious preaching.

9. THE SCORPION LADY

I'd pretty much had my fill of India, and I figured that I'd use Bainbridge's reward to get as far away from it as I could. It turned out that his notion of "generous" and mine differed considerably, and when the dust had cleared I found I only had enough money to fly to Siam.

I landed in Bangkok, found out that most of the white folks stayed at the Oriental Hotel, checked into a room there, and then set out to find some sinners that were more in need of redemption than most.

This led me to the Lumpini Stadium, where they were holding their nightly kick-boxing tournament, and when I heard that one of the combatants was named Moses I figured it was a signal from my Silent Partner and I put all my remaining money on him with one of the local bookmakers, and sure enough Moses kicked the bejabbers out of his opponent, and suddenly I had about six hundred dollars in my pocket, and I figured as long as God was looking over my shoulder there was no reason why I shouldn't let my money keep working for me.

A couple of discreet inquiries led me to the Scorpion Club a few blocks away. It had an exotic-looking doorway, and inside there was a long bar, a bunch of itinerant belly-dancers, and a few gaming tables, and before trying my luck I decided to slake my thirst on something with just enough alcohol to kill any germs I might have picked up during the day.

"Good evening, Father," said a voice at my left, and I turned to see that a nattily-dressed Englishman had sat down next to me.

"It's Reverend," I said. "The Reverend Lucifer Jones, at your service."

"Reginald McCorkle," he said, extending his hand. "It's very rare that one meets a man of the cloth in these surroundings."

"Trolling for sinners is a lot like trolling for fish," I explained. "You got to go where they congregate."

"Makes sense, at that," he agreed. "Will you allow me to buy you a drink?"

"I suppose I could hold my natural generosity in check long enough to accept your kind offer," I allowed. "You work around here, Brother McCorkle?"

He nodded. "And yourself?"

"I just stepped off the plane this afternoon," I said.

"You're staying at the Oriental, I presume?"

"Yeah," I said. "It's a nice enough temporary residence, until I decide where to build my tabernacle."

"It's about three miles away from here," he noted. "How did you happen to find this place?"

"It was highly recommended as a prime source of lost souls," I answered.

I was about to tell him about the kick-boxing, but just then the door opened and the most beautiful lady I ever did see walked in. She was Eurasian, and dressed in a slinky black gown, and she was wearing a necklace made of enormous pink pearls, and she had a huge jeweled scorpion pinned to her dress right between her lungs, and she had so many rings on her fingers that I figured it must have kept a diamond mine working all year around just supplying the stones for them. She glanced at me and Reginald McCorkle for just a second, and then walked over to a staircase and up to the second floor.

"Close your mouth, Reverend Jones," said McCorkle. "You never know what might fly into it in a place like this."

"I don't want to cut short an enjoyable conversation, Brother Reginald," I said, "but I think I've just been smitten by Cupid's capricious arrow."

"She does have that effect on people," said McCorkle.

"You know her?" I asked.

"I think just about everyone in Siam knows her, or at least knows of her," he replied.

"What's her name?"

"She has more names than you can shake a stick at," said Mc-Corkle. "In this part of the world she's known as the Scorpion Lady."

"She gets around a lot, does she?" I asked.

"Quite a lot."

"Good," I said. "We can compare travel notes once we get to know each other."

"You don't want to get to know her, Reverend Jones," continued McCorkle. "She's the most dangerous woman in all of Southeast Asia."

"A pretty little lady like that?" I said disbelievingly.

He nodded. "She runs the biggest smuggling operation in Siam, and is probably responsible for half the murders in Bangkok. She's so powerful that even the notorious Doctor Aristotle Ho gives her territory a wide berth."

"So what you're saying is that she's probably *not* responsible for half the murders in Bangkok," I said, trying to look on the bright side.

"She owns this club," added McCorkle. "It's her headquarters whenever she's in the country."

"How do *you* know all this, Brother Reginald?" I asked him.

"It's common knowledge. Ask anyone—or read a newspaper."

"Well, I thank you for all this advice," I said, "and for the drink as well, but my heart's been overcome by the siren song of true love."

"I warn you, Reverend," he said. "She's more than just a pretty face."

"I know," I said. "She's got one of the finest sets of lungs it's ever been my rare privilege to encounter."

I figured any further conversation would just depress me, so I took my leave of him then and headed over to the stairway, and when no one tried to stop me, I climbed up to the second floor. There was a door opposite the stairs with a light coming out from under it, so I walked up to it and knocked.

"Enter," said the most melodious voice I ever heard, and I pushed the door open.

She was sitting in front of a mirror, kind of admiring herself, which is just what I'd have done if I was her, and suddenly she spotted me in the mirror and turned to face me. "Who are you?" she demanded.

"I'm the Honorable Right Reverend Doctor Lucifer Jones, Miss Scorpion Lady, ma'am, and I've come to tell you that you are the most beautiful sight to grace my eyes since I landed on this continent some four years ago, and also to inquire delicately as to your current marital status."

She just stared at me for a minute without saying a word. Then she smiled. "How flattering, Doctor Jones."

"Ma'am, you got a voice like unto a symphony," I said. "Every word is a thing of undying beauty."

"Won't you have a seat, Doctor Jones?" said the Scorpion Lady.

"Thank you, ma'am, I sure will," I said, plopping myself down on a dainty little chair that had all kinds of mother-of-pearl designs inset in it. "And you can call me Lucifer."

"Thank you, Lucifer," she said. "And you may call me the Scorpion Lady."

"Just as a non sequitur, ma'am, ain't it scorpions that eat their husbands at a most indelicate point in their connubial relationship?"

"No, those are black widow spiders, Lucifer," she replied. "Why?"

"Oh, no reason in particular, ma'am," I said. "I was just kind of curious why such a gorgeous little lady, with a face like an angel and a tiny waistline and all other kinds of attributes would call herself the Scorpion Lady while some real high-class names like Fifi and Fatima are going begging."

"I have a passion for scorpions," she replied. "As you can see, most of my jewelry is shaped into facsimiles of them."

"And mighty fine jewelry it is, ma'am," I said, "though it pales into insignificance compared to your own beauty."

"I do believe you are trying to make me blush, Lucifer," she said with a smile.

"I ain't never seen an Oriental lady blush before," I answered. "It might be a pretty interesting and educational experience."

"Some other time," she said.

"Your wish is my command," I said. "You just name that other time and I'll be here with bells on."

"Why in the world would you want to wear bells?" she asked.

"That's just a figure of speech, ma'am," I explained. "Actually, what I'm trying to say is that you've won me over heart and soul."

"What if I don't *want* you, heart and soul?" she asked.

"That ain't my problem, ma'am," I said. "I had enough trouble just finding you and falling in love. I don't hardly see that making *you* fall in love too can rightly be considered my responsibility."

"You have an interesting notion of romancing a woman, Lucifer," she said.

"I'm just here to announce my feelings and intentions," I said. "The romancing comes a little later, after I've run my bankroll up at your tables downstairs. Though," I added, "if you want to get a head start on the romancing, I got no serious objections to that. I could bring us up a couple of beers and lock the door behind me."

"I'm afraid I'm a bit busy right now."

"No problem," I said. "I can come back in an hour or two, after you've slipped into something more comfortable, like maybe the bedroom."

"Is this the way you sweep them off their feet in America?" she asked with a smile.

"Well, truth to tell, ma'am, I ain't been back to America in quite some time, and I ain't never encountered an American girl with your virtues. Or if she had 'em, they sure as hell weren't in the same places."

"I assume that's a compliment," she said.

"No, ma'am," I said. "It's a statement of absolute fact. I know you got your detractors here in Bangkok, but I ain't one of 'em."

"Oh?" she said. "And who *are* my detractors?"

"Well, one of 'em is an English feller named Reginald McCorkle, who was buying me drinks down in the bar until I was smitten by your rare and exotic beauty."

"What did Reginald McCorkle tell you?"

"Nothing important," I said. "Probably he just wants you for himself, which is an understandable but unacceptable position."

She stared at me for a long moment, while I stared right back, my attention kind of torn betwixt her jewelry and her lungs.

"You are the most interesting man I have encountered in years, Lucifer," she said at last. "I do believe I shall let you pay court to me."

"I *knew* you couldn't say no to a good-looking young buck like me!" I said happily. "And being as how I'm a man of the cloth, it'll likely do wonders for your reputation too."

"There are a few ground rules we have to agree to, Lucifer," she said.

I wasn't aware that sex had any different ground rules in Siam than anywhere else in the world, but I perked up and paid attention, just so I wouldn't break no local taboos and wind up in the hoosegow while the Scorpion Lady wasted away grieving after me.

"I do not tolerate any competition," she said. "If you make a commitment to me, you make it willingly and totally."

"You got it," I said. "Should I get the drinks now?"

"I'm not finished," she said. "I also pledge to make a total commitment. If we are to become romantically involved, everything I have is yours." She paused. "That includes my nightclub, my house, my business interests, everything."

"I suppose I could adjust to that," I allowed.

"From this moment on, you are a full partner, Lucifer," she said. "In fact, I think that, starting tomorrow morning, I will turn my import-export business over to you."

"Well, that's mighty generous of you, Scorpion Lady," I said. "And I promise you won't be sorry you done it."

She got to her feet. "As I said, I have business to attend to tonight, but why don't you come back at, shall we say, six o'clock in the morning?"

"I'll bring my toothbrush, my pajamas, and me," I promised.

She walked me to the door, then grabbed me and gave me one of the more memorable kisses I'd ever got from a gorgeous lady smuggler, and then I was out in the hall and I heard the door lock behind me.

I climbed down the stairs, and walked over to the bar for a celebratory drink, and found Reginald McCorkle still sitting there.

"Well?" he said.

"Brother Reginald," I said, "you were dead wrong. She's the sweetest, prettiest, friendliest flower in all of Siam's gardens."

"I take it you hit it off with her?"

"You might say that."

"It's too bad," he said.

"You may have seen her first," I said, "but I spoke up first. Try to be a good loser, Brother Reginald."

"I don't plan to be any kind of loser at all, Reverend," he replied.

"You're too late," I said. "She's head over heels in love with me."

He pulled out his wallet and flashed a couple of official-looking cards at me. "Do you know what this means?" he said.

"It means you're a civil service employee," I answered.

"Read it carefully, Reverend Jones," he said. "I am in charge of the British High Commission in Siam. We've been after the Scorpion Lady for three years."

"That ain't none of my concern," I said.

"I hope to make it your concern," he said. "I want to enlist your help."

"Out of the question, Brother Reginald," I said. "I love her with a mad and all-encompassing passion."

"I just want you to consider it."

"Never," I said. "She's the heart of my heart and soul of my soul."

"I should add that there's a million-pound reward for any information leading to her capture and conviction," he said.

"On the other hand, she's just a woman," I said. "I can always get more."

He grinned. "I knew I could appeal to your better nature. When are you seeing her again?"

"Six in the morning."

"I'll tell you what," he said. "I'll be waiting in that little restaurant across the street. As soon as you leave here, come over and we'll discuss what you've learned."

Well, I figured the best he could expect was a lecture on whatever Oriental love techniques I learned, but I agreed to meet with him, and then I started walking back to the hotel, but a couple of ladies of the evening stopped me and struck up a conversation, and I decided that by the time I got to the hotel I'd just have to turn around and walk right back to the Black Scorpion, and besides I couldn't see that my pledge of eternal fidelity officially took effect until six in the morning, so one thing kind of led to another, and I left their company at about five o'clock, feeling mightily refreshed and ready to seize the day at such time as it should make an appearance.

I was banging away at the door to the Black Scorpion at six on the dot, and the Scorpion Lady clambered down the stairs and let me in.

"Here I am in all my masculine glory," I told her. "You ready to play Romeo and Juliet, or have you got something more exotic and Oriental in mind?"

"Ah, Lucifer," she said sadly, "I wish that I had time to introduce you to the more esoteric delights of the flesh, but we have a business to run. It will simply have to wait."

"It will?" I said.

She nodded. "You are in charge of my import-export business, remember?" she said.

"I had in mind something more in the way of importing a little ecstasy to you and exporting the memories of a brief but happy encounter with me when I left here," I said.

"Tonight," she promised me. "But for now, you have work to do."

"Tonight for sure?"

"For sure," she said.

"Okay," I said. "What do I have to do?"

"In the alley behind the Black Scorpion you will find an empty truck with the keys in the ignition," she said. "I want you to take it to the Acme Fertilizer Company on Phaya Tai Road and pick up a shipment from them."

"A shipment of what?"

"Fertilizer, of course," she said. "Then drive to the river and pull up to the Scorpion Freight Company."

"And then what?" I asked.

She smiled. "That's all. Just leave the truck there and come home. They'll unload it and return it tonight."

"Let me get this straight," I said. "I pick up a load of fertilizer from Acme, I drive it over to your shipping company, and that's *everything*?"

"That's right."

"Son of a gun," I said. "I thought there was more to running a million-dollar business than that. I'll be here by noontime."

"*You* may be," she said, "but I won't be back until nine in the evening. I'll be waiting for you then."

"You won't have long to wait," I promised her.

"All right," she said, starting to shut the door. "I'll see you then, Lucifer."

"As long as I got all day, I don't suppose there's no harm in my going across the street and grabbing a little breakfast first," I said.

"None at all," she said. "Until tonight, my love."

"Till tonight, my...uh...scorpion," I replied, and then I moseyed across the street and sat myself down at a table. Reginald McCorkle pulled up a chair a minute later.

"Well?" he said.

"I got to pick up a shipment of fertilizer at the Acme Fertilizer Company and deliver it to the Scorpion Freight Company," I told him.

"When?" he asked.

"No particular time," I said. "Long as I deliver it before dark, there ain't no problem."

"That's it?" he said. "No other pick-ups, no stops in between?"

"That's it."

"Then we've got her!" he exclaimed. "You'll drive directly to Acme, fill up the truck by seven o'clock, and then take it to a secret warehouse that I've leased on Set Siri Road. We'll have almost ten hours to discover what she's smuggling before you have to drive to her freight office. This is the break we've been waiting for, Reverend Jones!"

"I got a special request, Brother Reginald," I said.

"What is it?"

"Whatever we find, don't arrest her before midnight."

"Oh? Why not?"

"I got a romantic assignation arranged for nine o'clock tonight, and I'd hate to see the love of my life get marched off to the hoosegow without a chance at one last fling with a handsome and caring young man like myself."

"All right, Reverend Jones," he said. "It's a deal. We've been trying to arrest her for three years; I suppose an extra few hours won't make all that much difference. Now we'd best be started."

"After I eat breakfast," I said. "And since I'm working for the British High Commission, I think it's only fair and fitting that you pick up the check."

"All right, but be quick about it."

Well, so as not to cause him undue consternation, I ate a light breakfast consisting of nothing but orange juice and oatmeal and steak and eggs and hash browns and toast and biscuits and a few cups of coffee, and then I went into the alley behind the Black Scorpion and found this beautiful brand-new truck waiting for me. Sure enough, the keys were in the ignition, just like the Scorpion Lady had promised, and I drove out to Phaya Tai Road and cruised up and down it till I finally found the Acme Fertilizer Company. I backed up to one of their shipping docks, and before I could even tell 'em who I was or what I wanted, they began loading the truck up with bag after bag of fertilizer, and after about twenty minutes, when it was filled to the brim, they had me sign for it and then I was on my way again.

I spotted Reginald McCorkle's car waiting for me just outside the fertilizer factory, and I followed him to the warehouse he had leased on Set Siri Road, and pulled into it behind him. He closed the door and turned on the lights while I climbed out of the cab of the truck.

"What now?" I asked him.

"Now we start examining your cargo and see what she's trying to smuggle out of the country."

"Surely you got a staff to do that kind of menial labor, ain't you?" I asked.

"No," he said. "There was no one I could be sure I could trust. There's just you and me, Reverend." He unbuttoned his shirt cuffs and rolled up his sleeves. "Let's get to work."

We each pulled a bag of fertilizer out of the back of the truck, and he tossed me a knife.

"Open them very carefully along the tops," he said, "so that we can close them when we're through and no one will know that they've been examined."

I did as he said, and poured the contents out on the dirt floor.

"What have you got there?" he asked, while working on his own bag.

"Looks like about fifty pounds of elephant shit to me," I said. "Smells like it, too."

"Sift through it carefully," he told me. "There could be a bag of drugs or diamonds in the very middle of it."

"Sift through it with *what*?" I asked.

"Your fingers, of course," he said, kneeling down and going to work on his own pile.

After five minutes we had both determined that the bags contained exactly what they were supposed to contain, and nothing else.

"Ah, she's a sly devil, that one!" said McCorkle, never losing his enthusiasm. "Probably only one or two bags contain the goods."

"You ain't seriously suggesting that after we pick all this stuff up and throw it back into the bags and seal 'em up that we do the same thing all over again with the other seventy or eighty bags?" I said.

"Do you know a better way?" he demanded.

"Not offhand," I said. "But that don't mean there ain't one."

"More work and less talk," he said, pulling another bag off the truck. "Just keep thinking of the reward."

Well, I spent the next five hours thinking of the reward, and the three hours after that thinking of a bath, and by the time four o'clock rolled around we had to admit that what I had in my truck was a few tons of elephant shit and nothing else.

"Probably this was just a test run," he said when we'd gotten 'em all loaded back into the truck. "Once you deliver it and show up back at the Black Scorpion, she'll know she can trust you. To-morrow you'll pick up the real stuff. I'll be waiting for you in the restaurant again."

Well, I drove on down to the river, and spent about an hour hunting up the Scorpion Freight Company, and then I left the truck there like she had told me to, and walked the four or five miles back to my hotel. I'd done more lifting and working than I'd done in years, and I ached everywhere, and I took a long hot bath and finally stopped smelling like an elephant about halfway through it.

I showed up at the Black Scorpion club a little after nine, and dragged myself up the stairs to the Scorpion Lady's room.

"You look terrible, Lucifer," she said.

"It's been a long, hard day," I said. "We'll get around to the han-ky-panky in a couple of minutes, but first I just gotta lie down here for a second."

I walked over to her bed and collapsed on it, and the next thing I knew she was shaking my shoulder and telling me that it was six in the morning and it was time to take the truck back to the Acme Fertilizer Company and make another pick-up.

I walked over to the restaurant, all bleary-eyed, had my usual modest breakfast with a little more coffee than usual, and an hour later Reginald McCorkle and me were sifting through another five tons of elephant shit, looking for the elusive contraband that the Scorpion Lady was smuggling out of the country. Once again we didn't find it.

Well, this went on for the better part of two weeks, us examin-ing tons of elephant shit every day, and me falling asleep on the Scorpion Lady's bed every night before we could get around to con-summating our romance, and just about the time I was ready to call it quits and give up on the reward and just spend the next few years enjoying a little pre-connubial bliss, she told me that I was all through going to Acme Fertilizer Company and would now be making my pick-ups at the Prime Fish Hatcheries.

"Excellent news!" said Reginald while I was eating my breakfast. "Now we're getting somewhere! I had thought that the first day was a test, but obviously she is a very careful woman. She sent you there fourteen days in a row before she knew she could trust you, and now we're finally going to pick up her contraband goods."

The truck was waiting for me in the alley, all cleaned and polished and looking like new, as usual, and I drove it over to the Prime Fish Hatcheries, where they loaded it up, and half an hour later me and Reginald were in his warehouse, looking at maybe twenty thousand dead fish.

"Damn, but she's a clever one!" he muttered.

"She is?"

"Obviously she's put the goods inside one or more of the fish, but only her contact can tell which ones. We'll just have to cut them open one by one until we come to whatever it is we're looking for."

Well, we spent ten hours looking through fish guts for diamonds or microfilms or opium, and mostly what we found were fish guts. I smelled worse than ever when I left the truck at her freight office and trudged back to the hotel, and it took longer than usual to wash all the odors away, and as a result I didn't have no time for dinner before I showed up at the Black Scorpion, and I was so tired and weak from hunger that this time I didn't even climb the stairs and fall asleep in her bed, but instead I sat down at the bar to catch my breath and the next thing I knew the sun was shining in and the Scorpion Lady was shaking me awake, and then I gobbled some breakfast and me and Reginald spent another day cutting fish open with no hint of success.

Two weeks later the Scorpion Lady told me to skip the Hatchery and go back to the Acme Fertilizer Company, and Reginald attacked the elephant shit with the same enthusiasm he had attacked it a month earlier. As for me, I was discovering that the life of a millionaire businessman wasn't all it was cracked up to be, and I made up my mind that the next morning at breakfast I was calling it quits and spending the next few years romancing the true love of my life.

That night I was so tired that I didn't even make it out of my hotel. I fell asleep in the tub, woke up when the water got cold, and barely made it to my bed before I fell asleep again. I got up at about five thirty in the morning and hopped a cab over to the Black Scorpion. It was locked, and I figured the Scorpion Lady must have had a pretty hard night too, because no matter how much I banged on the door nobody came down the stairs to let me in.

Finally I decided to go across the street and grab some breakfast and give Reginald my notice, but when I got there I couldn't spot him, so I just sat down and had the waiter bring me the usual.

I was just polishing off the last of my steak and eggs when a well-dressed Englishman walked over and sat down across from me.

"Are you Lucifer Jones?" he asked.

"The Right Reverend Doctor Lucifer Jones," I corrected him. "And who are you?"

"My name is Winston Spiggot," he said. "I work for the British High Commission."

"Did Reginald McCorkle send you?" I asked.

"Reginald McCorkle is in no position to send anyone anywhere," he replied. "In fact, even as we speak he is being sent home in black disgrace."

"You don't say," I said. "What all did he do?"

"He bungled his assignment, and let the Scorpion Lady escape."

"Escape?" I said. "What are you talking about?"

"She fled the country during the night, when she got word that I had replaced McCorkle. I missed her by no more than an hour."

"I don't suppose she left no forwarding address?" I said, trying to soothe my broken heart.

"Don't be foolish, Doctor Jones," he said. "A number of people at the High Commission wanted me to take you into custody, but as I see it you were simply an unwitting dupe." He paused. "Nonetheless, you have caused us a great deal of trouble, and I think it might be best for all concerned were you also to leave Siam."

"Well, with the love of my life on the lam, I can't see no compelling reason to stay here," I said. "But I think you guys have got her figured all wrong. Me and Reginald went over every truckload of fertilizer and dead fish with a fine-tooth comb, and I guarantee she wasn't smuggling nothing out of the country."

"Certainly she was," said Winston Spiggot. "I wouldn't expect you to have figured it out, but McCorkle was a professional. He should have known."

"What was it?" I asked. "Something in the fish or something in the elephant shit?"

"Neither."

"You mean it was the fish and the fertilizer themselves?"

"Idiot!" he said. "You helped her smuggle twenty-nine brand-new armored trucks to Doctor Aristotle Ho's army!"

It was with a heavy heart that I took a boat down the Chao Phraya River to the ocean that afternoon and hopped the next ship north for Japan, where I planned to forget the duplicitous love of my life in the arms of as many Geisha girls as my anguished soul and bankroll could mutually accommodate at one time.

10. THE OTHER MASTER DETECTIVE

It took the ship the better part of five days to reach Japan, by which time I was more than happy to take my leave of it, especially since the cabin girl with whom I wiled away a couple of pleasant afternoons happened to have a brother on the crew who took an instant dislike to me for no discernable reason, and spent half of the last evening hunting for me with a Samurai sword while I huddled in a lifeboat and counted off the last few hours until we hit shore.

Tokyo was one of the more crowded cities I ever saw. I've been mulling on it all these years now, and I think the reason is that they've got too many people crowding into too few streets, and if I ever go back I plan to tell the Emperor, or whoever's in charge these days, that it'd be a good idea to move some of 'em out to the suburbs.

Still, I was young and adventurous back then, and it didn't bother me none, because the more people there were, the more likely I was to find some who didn't mind sharing their money with an upstanding man of the cloth who was all ready to settle down and build his tabernacle and get to work on his life's calling.

There wasn't a lot of white folks in Japan in those days, and them that found themselves there split their loyalties between the Imperial Hotel and the Nikkatsu Hotel, and since the Nikkatsu was closer to the Ginza and had the biggest gaming room in town, I made a beeline toward it.

"Have you any luggage, Mr. Jones?" asked the desk clerk after I'd signed in.

"That's *Reverend* Jones, and no, I ain't got naught but the clothes on my back, me being a servant of God and all," I said.

"Then I am afraid I must ask if you can afford to pay for your room," he said.

I flashed him my six hundred dollars, which I hadn't touched since the kick-boxing matches in Siam, and he looked much relieved.

"Excellent, Reverend Jones," he said. "Will you be wanting a room with or without?"

"With or without what?" I asked.

"With or without a Geisha."

"With, I think," I said. "They tend to brighten up a room, don't you agree?"

He marked something down on my form. "Do you want a single or a double?"

"I didn't know Geishas came in different sizes," I replied. "I'll have to spend a moment or two considering it."

"I meant a single or a double room, Reverend Jones," said the desk clerk.

A single room sounded like I'd expend less energy chasing her around it, so that was what I asked for.

"Fine," he said. "A bellboy will be by to show you to your room in just a moment. And if you would like anything at all, just ask."

"Well, you might recommend a good restaurant," I said.

"I'd be happy to," he answered. "The Momonjiya, just across the street, specializes in monkey brains. If you find that too exotic for your taste, then go to the Taiko down the block."

"The Taiko, huh? What do *they* serve?"

"The sexual organs of oxen, highly spiced."

"Don't anyone around here cook no hamburgers?" I demanded.

He looked shocked. "Please, not so loud, Reverend Jones. We don't wish to offend the clientele."

Well, I'd kind of lost my appetite during the conversation anyway, so I followed the bellhop to the staircase and up two flights to the third floor, where we walked down to the end of the hall, and he unlocked my door and kind of stood there jingling his change in his pocket, but since I hadn't had any luggage for him to tote I just laid my hand on his head and blessed him, and he walked off muttering to himself in Japanese.

I entered my room and took a look around. The bed wasn't much—it was a pile of silks on a wood board—but it beat the hell out of the furniture, which was more to look at than sit on. There was a knock at the door, and I figured it was the bellhop back to argue about the tip, but when I opened it the cutest little Geisha girl I ever set eyes on entered the room and minced over to the window.

"You have a beautiful view here," she said in a voice that was a lot deeper than anyone looking at her would have expected.

"Well, now that you're here, I got *two* beautiful views," I said. "What's your name, Honey?"

"Miyoshi," she said, turning around and facing me.

"Well, that's a right pretty name," I said. "And you can call me Lucifer."

"Would you perhaps like a massage before your bath?" said Miyoshi.

I walked over to her. "How's about we indulge in a little mutual massaging?" I said.

I think I reached out to her to demonstrate what I meant, but things happened awfully fast then and it's kind of hard to remember. All I know is that about two seconds later I was flying through the air, and I landed on my back with a thud, and Miyoshi was kneeling on top of me with her fists doubled up and growling kind of deep in her throat.

"I guess I got to work on my timing, huh?" I muttered.

"I'm sorry," said Miyoshi, and now her voice was yet another octave lower and most of her accent was gone. "It was a reflex action."

"You got the healthiest reflexes I ever encountered, Miyoshi," I said. "Now how's about hopping off my chest? I'm having trouble breathing."

"My name isn't Miyoshi," said the Geisha, standing up and removing her wig, and I saw now that she was a man. "I am sorry for the deception, but it was necessary."

"You're a Geisha *boy*?" I said, getting painfully to my feet. "I didn't know they came in both flavors."

He shook his head. "I am Toshiro Mako of Interpol," he said. "Perhaps you have heard of me?"

"I'm afraid not," I said. "The only Oriental detective I know is Inspector Willie Wong of the Hong Kong Police."

"That bumbling incompetent, with his stupid platitudes and his legion of apelike children!" said Mr. Mako contemptuously.

"You ain't on real good terms with him, I take it?"

"*I* am a master of disguise," said Mr. Mako. "I speak seventeen languages, possess a black belt in karate, and hold the Chair of Antiquities at Pacific University in my spare time, but do *I* ever get any publicity? No, it's always that Hong Kong clown with his pigeon English and his idiot parables! He always gets the best cases!" Suddenly his eyes flashed with triumph. "But *this* time will be different! This time I, Mr. Mako, will make headlines the world over!"

"For impersonating a Geisha girl?" I said. "Them ain't exactly the kind of headlines designed to endear you to the public, Mr. Mako."

He shook his head. "This is just a disguise, Doctor Jones," he explained. "My quarry has a room down the hall, and I am keeping him under surveillance, just waiting for the opportune moment to strike."

"Who are you after?" I asked him.

"Have you ever heard of Doctor Aristotle Ho, the Insidious Oriental Dentist?" he said.

"The name ain't totally unfamiliar to me," I said. "Is *he* staying here at the Nikkatsu?"

Mr. Mako nodded his head. "Yes. He's got some criminal coup in mind. I haven't been able to determine what it is, but I plan to dog his steps night and day, and when he makes his move, I shall make mine."

"He's already wanted all over Asia," I said. "Why don't you just arrest him now and cart him off to the calaboose?"

"I want his entire organization," said Mr. Mako as a kind of fanatical glow spread across his face. "*Then* let them talk about Willie Wong!"

"Well, I wish you all the luck in the world, Mr. Mako," I said. "But I think I'm gonna move over to the Imperial Hotel just to get out of the line of fire, so to speak." I reached out a hand. "It's been nice meeting you."

"I'm afraid I can't permit that, Doctor Jones," he said. "Any sudden unexplained activity could draw Doctor Ho's attention."

"I'll explain it at the desk," I said. "I'll just say that I was looking for something in the way of a blonde Geisha girl."

He shook his head. "I can't run the risk of alerting him. You will have to stay here." He paused. "In fact, I may have to impress you into service."

"What are you talking about?"

"I can't keep watching him every moment of the night and day," said Mr. Mako. "Even I have to sleep and eat and answer calls of Nature. Yes, the more I think about it, the more I see that I need your help."

"I don't know about this…" I said reluctantly.

"Think of the publicity, Doctor Jones!" he said. "Not only will we rid the world of this vermin, but we'll push Inspector Willie Wong off the front page!"

"I ain't got nothing against Willie Wong," I protested. "And now that I come to think of it, I ain't got nothing against Doctor Aristotle Ho, neither."

"Do you have anything against rewards?"

"I got a lot against risking life and limb for 'em," I said.

"That won't be necessary," said Mr. Mako. "You just follow him when I'm unavailable. Take notes of where he goes and who he meets, and keep out of sight. I'll take over from there."

"You're *sure* that's all I gotta do?" I said.

"Absolutely," said Mr. Mako. "I'm willing to share the reward with you, but I want the glory of capturing him myself. I'll show the world you don't need twenty-eight sons and a handful of trite aphorisms to be Asia's finest detective!"

Well, he seemed pretty sincere to me, so I finally agreed, provided that when it was all over he'd also tell the world that he was just in disguise as a Geisha girl and he and I didn't have no degenerate relationship going on behind the scenes, and then he went to sleep on the couch and left the bed for me, but about two in the morning I finally decided that I had to get something to eat even if it meant eating at the Momonjiya or the Taiko, so I climbed into my clothes and tiptoed out into the hall so as not to wake the sleeping Mr. Mako, and then I climbed down the stairs and headed out the door of the hotel into the street, figuring I'd just walk up and down the row of restaurants until I came to one with some civilized food in the window, and then suddenly I saw a familiar-looking figure walking ahead of me, and I realized that it was Doctor Aristotle Ho.

I hid in the shadows until he got a little farther away from me, and then fell into step behind him and followed him for about a mile, and suddenly we were in the Ginza, and every building was either a casino or a bar or a drug den or a whorehouse, and while it made me feel right at home, I didn't dare relax or partake in none of the entertainments with the Insidious Oriental Dentist just ahead of me. Finally he turned into a small tavern, and I stopped about fifty feet away and decided to wait till he came out rather than go in after him.

Suddenly I heard some gunshots coming from the tavern, and then there was a scream, and then a whole bunch of little yellow fellers raced out, and a crowd started gathering around the place, and then Doctor Ho walked out, calm as you please, with a smoking pistol in his hand. He tucked it into the belt of his brocaded robe, looked contemptuously at the crowd, all of whom backed away, and then turned to his right and started walking away.

One little old gray-haired Japanese feller stepped out of the crowd and started following him, and I walked over and grabbed him by the shoulder.

"Hey, neighbor," I said, "you don't want to get involved. That's the notorious Doctor Aristotle Ho."

He yelled something in Japanese at me, and I hung on to his arm.

"He shoots people for a livelihood," I explained. "Leave this to the authorities and maybe you won't get your damnfool head blown off."

Well, by now Doctor Ho had heard the commotion, and he turned and recognized me, and pulled out his pistol and fired twice, just as I pulled the old Japanese guy to the ground. When I looked up again, he was gone.

"Fool!" muttered the old guy. "I had him within my grasp!"

He started pulling off his mustache and wig, and suddenly I was looking at Mr. Mako.

"Why the hell didn't you tell me it was you?" I demanded.

"He would have overheard."

"What are you doing here in the first place?" I said. "I left you sleeping back at the hotel."

"I heard you leave," said Mr. Mako, "and since I couldn't be sure that Doctor Ho hadn't seen through my Geisha disguise, I thought I'd better come along to protect you."

"Don't you ever go anywhere as just plain Mr. Mako?" I asked.

He shook his head. "I am much too famous. Only my ability as a master of disguise allows me the freedom of movement."

A couple of bystanders had been watching him as he plucked off his mustache and wig and got rid of his cane, and one of them walked up.

"May I have your autograph?" he said.

"You see?" said Mr. Mako to me. "It happens everywhere I go."

"I've followed all your cases from Honolulu to Tokyo, Inspector Wong," continued the man. "What brings you to our fair city?"

Mr. Mako started cursing a blue streak, and didn't stop until the autograph seeker had run off in fear of his life.

"Come on, Mr. Mako," I said when he had finally run out of breath. "It's just been one of those days. I'll buy you a beer."

"Saki," he said.

"What's that?" I asked. "A Japanese brand?"

He just glared at me and walked into the nearest bar, and he didn't start loosening up until he'd had his fourth or fifth saki, which is this Oriental beer with no head on it that they serve in tiny little glasses.

"I was so close," he murmured. "So close!"

"Well, the thing to remember, Mr. Mako," I said, "is that Doctor Ho was just as close to you, and he was the one with the gun. Besides," I added, "he was all alone, and you said you wanted his whole gang."

"His *whole* gang encompasses entire armies and governments," said Mr. Mako. "What I meant was that I wanted his Japanese operatives."

"What's he doing here anyway?" I asked. "I thought he operated on the mainland."

Mr. Mako shrugged. "That is something else we have to discover, but I suspect that it involves our pearl industry."

"You grow a lot of pearls in Japan, do you?" I asked.

"You make it sound like you think they grow on trees, Doctor Jones," he said, amused.

"Nonsense," I said. "Everyone knows you dig for 'em in mines."

He just stared at me for a minute and then continued. "Recently we heard through the underworld grapevine that a criminal mastermind was planning to steal our entire supply of pearls. Doctor Ho's presence here would seem to confirm it."

"Where do you keep all your pearls, Mr. Mako?" I asked.

"In a building—a fortress, really—called the Pearl Exchange, on the edge of Shiba Park, right next to the ancient Buddhist Temple. It is there that Doctor Ho will strike."

"Well, then, it's just as well he got away tonight, ain't it?" I said.

"You are quite right, Doctor Jones," he said. "In my enthusiasm I moved too soon. I owe you an apology."

"Happily accepted," I said. "Now why don't we get on back to the hotel and grab forty or fifty winks?"

"You go ahead," he said. "I am wide awake now, and perhaps it would be best for me to do some reconnoitering."

I didn't put up no objections, especially since he had left his Geisha duds back in the hotel, and I figured it wouldn't enhance neither of our reputations to be seen going into my room together, so I left him there and returned to the Nikkatsu Hotel and was sound asleep and snoring to beat the band a couple of minutes later.

The room was still empty when I got up at noon, so I shaved and dressed and went out hunting for a little breakfast that didn't have no monkey brains or ox organs or dead fish in it, but I found that I couldn't read the menus, which were all printed in Japanese, so after walking into and out of three or four restaurants I finally sat myself down and pointed to a pot of tea, and settled for drinking my breakfast with a bit of milk and sugar.

It was only as I was pouring my second cup that I realized that the placed suddenly seemed a lot less crowded than it had, and as I looked up I saw all the customers and waiters and cashiers running for the door, and I figured the place must have caught fire or something, and I jumped to my feet to join them when a heavy hand landed on my shoulder and shoved me back down, and then the proud owner of the hand sat down and I found myself staring across the table at Doctor Aristotle Ho.

"We meet again, Doctor Jones," he said.

"Look," I said, "I'm right sorry that your temple collapsed and it put your plans of worldwide conquest on hold, but it wasn't my fault."

"Why do you continue to torment me, Doctor Jones?" he said. "No sooner do you leave Sir Mortimer's company in India than I find you in Tokyo, working in concert with Mr. Mako. What have you got against me?"

"Nothing," I said. "Cross my heart and hope to die."

"Be careful what you wish for, Doctor Jones," he said. "It may come true sooner than you think."

"The only reason I was with Mr. Mako was because I thunk he was a Geisha girl." He just stared coldly at me and didn't make no reply. "I guess that requires some further explanation, right?"

"I am in no mood for your drolleries, Doctor Jones," said Doctor Ho. "I have come here to ask you to deliver a message for me."

"A message?"

"I want you to tell Mr. Mako that if he persists in trying to thwart me, he will not survive the week."

"You'd make him a lot madder if you told him you were an admirer of Inspector Willie Wong's," I said helpfully.

"Just deliver the message."

"Right," I said.

"As for yourself," he continued, "this is the third time our paths have crossed."

"Well, it's the fourth time, actually," I said. "There was your farm in China, and then the secret sex ceremony in India, and then last night, and now this afternoon."

"Silence!" he snapped. "Do not contradict me when I am about to deliver an ultimatum."

"Okay," I said. "We just won't count last night, since it was an accident anyway."

"*Shut up!*" he screamed.

"Whatever you say."

He took a deep breath and continued. "That was the first time I have lost my temper in fifty-three years. You have a strange effect on me, Doctor Jones."

"You probably just ain't used to dealing with Christian gentlemen that was brung up to respect the Ten Commandments and the Bill of Rights and such," I said sympathetically.

"*Be quiet!*" he snapped, and then started blinking his eyes right fast. "I quite forgot what I was going to say."

"Beats me," I said. "So if you'll excuse me, I think I'll just be moseying back to my hotel now and—"

"Sit down and be still!" he said, still fighting to control his temper. "I have remembered what I had to say to you." He leaned across the table and stared into my eyes. "The next time our paths cross will be the last time."

"Well, I sure am relieved to hear that, Doctor Ho," I said. "I was afraid we were going to keep bumping into each other every few months for the rest of our lives. You planning on taking an extended trip somewhere?"

"You don't understand what I am saying to you," he said with a frown.

"Sure I do," I said. "You figure we're only gonna meet once more, and then I said that—"

"Can you possibly be this stupid, or is it all an act?" he interrupted.

"I resent that!"

"Never mind," he said wearily. "Just see to it that Mr. Mako receives my message."

"Happy to, Doctor Ho," I told him.

He got up and walked out of the restaurant, and suddenly all the customers and crew came back in, and the manager tore up my bill and just asked me to leave real quick, which I thought was a right gentlemanly thing of him to do simply because I'd attracted a local celebrity to his establishment, and I walked back to the hotel to deliver Doctor Ho's message to Mr. Mako, but the room was still empty.

I was about to go out in search of a friendly little game of chance, or maybe a Geisha who didn't change genders every time I turned around, when I saw a piece of paper lying on the table next to the phone, so I picked it up and read it:

Doctor Jones:
Pearl Exchange, 5:00 PM. The net is closing!
Mr. Mako

This put me in a bit of a quandary, since I knew Mr. Mako didn't want no help apprehending Doctor Ho, but on the other hand I thought the very least I should do as a law-abiding Christian gentleman was deliver Doctor Ho's message to him, so he could reconsider his plans if he was of a mind to protect life and limb and other vital organs.

I mulled on it for a couple of minutes, and finally went down to the front desk and asked where the Pearl Exchange was, but the directions were so complicated that I finally gave up and hired a rickshaw to take me there. It was maybe 4:30 when I arrived, which meant I had half an hour to find Mr. Mako before he went up against Doctor Ho.

The Pearl Exchange was a huge building which looked like it had withstood a lot of charges and sieges over the centuries before someone got the bright idea of stashing all of Japan's pearls there. There were bars on all the windows, and soldiers standing guard all around the place, and a bunch of English and American and Chinese and Arab merchants kept coming and going, and since I knew Mr. Mako was a master of disguise I scrutinized each and every one of them, trying to spot him, but within ten or fifteen minutes they had all left the building, and suddenly there wasn't no one left inside but me and an old Indian gentleman in a wheelchair and a uniformed Japanese feller standing guard on one of the balconies.

I checked my watch and saw that the doors were due to close in another few minutes, and then I finally realized that I was watching the Master of Disguise in action, and that the old Indian in the wheelchair was really Mr. Mako. I was about to walk up and congratulate him on his get-up, but I didn't want to give him away to Doctor Ho, who was probably lurking in the shadows somewhere, so I just stood back and admired him for a minute or two.

Then I saw a flash of motion out of the corner of my eye, and I looked up and saw that the uniformed guard was walking along the balcony to where he could get a clearer view of Mr. Mako, and that as he did so he unsnapped the leather cover on his holster and wrapped his fingers around the handle of his pistol.

I raced up the stairs just as he pulled his pistol out and was taking aim, and hit him with a tackle that under other circumstances would have got me a contract to play for the Chicago Bears.

"No!" I hollered. "You can't shoot him! That's Mr. Mako!"

We rolled along the floor a bit, and his gun got jarred loose, and then Mr. Mako jumped up out of his wheelchair and looked up at us and shook a fist in the air and ran out of there hell for leather, and suddenly I listened to the guard cursing and hollering at me and his voice sounded awfully familiar.

"Fool!" he screamed. "Idiot! Imbecile!" He ripped his eyebrows and beard and mustache off. "*I* am Mako! *That* was Doctor Aristotle Ho!"

"Well, how the hell was I to know?" I said.

"He is getting away, and it is all your fault!" yelled Mr. Mako. "Worse still, our informants tell us that his next port of call is Hong Kong. Now Inspector Willie Wong will get all the glory again!"

"It ain't my fault," I said. "I was just trying to protect you."

Well, poor Mr. Mako just broke down and cried, and I did my best to comfort him and explained that even though he'd lost Aristotle Ho he had saved the country's pearls, but he wouldn't have no part of it, and finally he got control of himself and insisted that I come with him to his car, and then he drove me to his office and told his secretary to bring him any file Interpol might have on me, and wouldn't let me light up a cigar or have a beer or nothing until she returned lugging this huge folder.

"You have been a busy man since you arrived in Asia, Doctor Jones," he said after he'd spent a few minutes reading what she'd brought him.

"Well, I try to keep active," I said.

"'Active' is an understatement," he said, still thumbing through the folder. "Not only did you help Doctor Aristotle Ho escape from me today, but it seems that you are wanted for setting up an illegal gambling operation in Macau."

"I didn't make a penny on that," I said defensively.

"Let me continue. The Chinese government has issued a warrant for your arrest for the murder of a General Chang."

"A simple misunderstanding," I said.

"Tibet is after you for absconding with a national treasure," he continued.

"He wasn't no national treasure," I protested. "He was just a basketball player on the lam from the mob. He wasn't even a Tibetan!"

"The government of India wants you for your complicity in the destruction of a national shrine, as well as killing eight tigers without a license," he said.

"I didn't kill 'em, I just sort of *appropriated* 'em," I said. "Well, seven of 'em, anyway."

"And the government of Siam has charged you with smuggling armored vehicles."

"I can explain all that," I said.

"And worst of all," he said, glaring at me, "when you were in Hong Kong you helped Willie Wong grab yet another headline!" He got to his feet and walked around to the front of his desk. "Speaking in my capacity as the chief representative of Interpol on the Asian continent, I must inform you that your presence here is no longer tolerable, Doctor Jones. I could, of course, turn you over to any of the governments that seek to bring you to trial, but relations between your country and my own have become strained recently, and I do not wish to exacerbate an already tense situation. Therefore, if you will sign a pledge agreeing never to return to Asia, I will put you on the Trans-Siberian Express and let you become Europe's headache."

"And if I don't sign it?" I asked.

"Then I will have to devise a series of coin tosses to determine which government gets to incarcerate you first. The choice is yours."

Well, it wasn't all that much of a choice that I could see, and I figured that if all my efforts to bring the word of the Lord to these brown and yellow heathen were that unappreciated, it was probably time for me to pull up stakes and take my leave of the place anyway, so I signed his paper and he flew me to Siberia, where I really could have used my pandaskin coat, and placed me on the train and pointed me to the West, and that was the end of my attempt to civilize the barbaric hordes of Asia.

Which ain't to say that my preaching days were over. During the next few years I came to grips with some mighty interesting folks and critters in the glittering capitals of Europe, and made and lost a fortune or two, and discovered a lost continent, and fell hopelessly and eternally in love fifteen or twenty times, and even was king of my own country for a spell.

But that is another story, and writing is mighty thirsty work.

ᔕ The End (Volume Two) ᘔ

CPSIA information can be obtained at www.ICGtesting.com
Printed in the USA
BVOW070705030512

289213BV00001B/86/P